Selected Poems

Geoff Cochrane

*Also by Geoff Cochrane*

POETRY

Images of Midnight City (1976)
Solstice (with Victoria Broome and Lindsay Rabbitt) (1979)
The Sea the Landsman Knows (1980)
Taming the Smoke (1983)
Kandinsky's Mirror (1989)
Aztec Noon: Poems 1976–1992 (1992)
Into India (1999)
Acetylene (2001)
Nine Poems (2002)
Vanilla Wine (2003)
Hypnic Jerks (2005)
84-484 (2007)
Pocket Edition (2009)
The Worm in the Tequila (2010)
The Bengal Engine's Mango Afterglow (2012)
Wonky Optics (2015)
RedEdits (2017)
The Black and the White (2019)
Chosen (2020)

NOVELS

Tin Nimbus (1995)
Blood (1997)

SHORT STORIES

Brindle Embers (2002)
White Nights (2004)
Astonished Dice: Collected Short Stories (2014)

# Selected Poems

GEOFF COCHRANE

TE HERENGA WAKA
UNIVERSITY PRESS

Te Herenga Waka University Press
Victoria University of Wellington
PO Box 600 Wellington
teherengawakapress.co.nz

A catalogue record is available at the National Library
of New Zealand.

ISBN 9781776921201

Printed in Singapore by Markono Print Media Pte Ltd

# Contents

# FOREWORD
## by Fergus Barrowman

Ashley Venus is working on a story. A dour fiction which refuses to unfold. His subject is sexual loneliness. A mistake of course – he's *writing a Big Mistake*.
    —*Jungle Altars* (unpublished novel, 1997)

Damien Wilkins' writer-at-work interview, published in *Sport* 31 in late 2003 and reprinted here, captures Geoff Cochrane at his peak, when he had in quick succession published the three essential books of poems – *Into India* (1999), *Acetylene* (2001), *Vanilla Wine* (2003) – in which his elegant and pungent voice is most fully realised.

But Damien also caught Geoff in the pits. He had spent the 1990s making himself into a novelist, and he had failed. A novella, *Quest Clinic*, was published in *Sport* in 1992, and the novels *Tin Nimbus* in 1995 and *Blood* in 1997. They received terrific reviews, and have ardent fans still, and there were film options and whatnot, but they sold like slender volumes of verse. Three further novels – *My Last Night on Earth*, *Carnival Rockets* and *Jungle Altars* – remain in manuscript. As best I can remember, this was not so much rejection as mutual decision by writer and publisher to wait until the time was right, or perhaps until we could imagine a different outcome. But the poetry came at a book every two years, until the novels were dimmed by time.

Five novels and a novella: six golden youths who fall prey to alcohol. Each variation on the theme is distinctive and engaging, but together they are more variations than you want. Bede, Sean and Grant; Abel Blood and Ashley Venus. The one that gives me pause as a failed publisher is John Grogan of *Carnival Rockets*. His progress is from schoolboy prodigy to pianist/comedian at Pedro's nightclub, and – after his finger is broken by a heavy and the club is destroyed by an arsonist, and stints in Auckland and Blackwater on the West Coast – back to a council flat in Wellington. At each station a hopeless sexual obsession, the last with a glamorous journalist who has interviewed him about his just-published and ignored first novel. "Writing a novel provided him with a reason for getting out of bed in the morning."

Out of this failure – out of these years of hard labour, and this astonishing recreation of Wellington from the Seventies to the Nineties, with its dusk- and dawn-coloured lights and floral and briny pongs, and its cast of crooks, counterfeiters, secret agents, barmaids and good keen women – spring the astonishing poems of *Into India* and the books that followed it.

I first met Geoff in 1991. He tells the story to Damien on page 30, and I'm sure he's right about how it happened, but I have no memory of being introduced to him by Lindsay Rabbitt at a book launch. What remains with me is the sensation of reading poems like 'An Ambulance' for the first time, but whether in a submission to *Sport* or in the manuscript of *Aztec Noon* I have no idea. In any case, half a dozen poems went into *Sport 7*, and the book appeared early the next year. What strikes me about *Aztec Noon* now is the change from the early poems – recognisably Geoff, but a little florid and self-conscious, a little submarine – to the vivid, measured precision of the new work.

I understood then that *Aztec Noon* was the product of Geoff's sobriety – the new poems, the assembly of the new-and-selected manuscript, the offer to VUP – and Lindsay's encouragement, just as Gerald Melling's friendship buoyed Geoff up in the threadbare twenty-first century. What I didn't understand was what sobriety really meant. Years later, Geoff told me that he still dreamed of drinking every night, and woke up in grief every morning. Rereading the thirteen collections of poems we published together, it comes up over and over.

Publishing Geoff was like stepping into a world I could almost remember. Manuscripts were typewritten. Gerry failed for years to teach him to use the laptop he had given him, until Geoff could no longer get a replacement ribbon for his beloved Brother. He learned how to get his poems onto his laptop, and would bring it into the office so that Craig Gamble could help him get them off again. Editorial notes were received with patience. Meetings were arranged by letter, or later by leaving a message on his cellphone, which he inconveniently couldn't answer or call back on. We would meet at the office – in which case Geoff would bring a discounted cake – or at establishments like the Paramount Cafeteria or the Pioneer Coffee Lounge or Kenny's Café, until they were all gone, and the Victoria Street Café (see pages 219, 222 and 226) had to fill in as a not very convincing period set.

Geoff has never been one of our bestsellers, but if he hasn't had the *most* readers he's had the *most fervent* readers, and I was enormously moved, as Geoff would have been, by the love shown by writers and readers in the days after his sudden and shocking death – a dateless death, because he was found in his Miramar flat. As James Brown said in his tribute, so many of us have had a Geoff Cochrane moment, which has stayed with us and changed us as readers. Sam Duckor-Jones offered a beautifully Cochrane-esque string of adjectives: "curly and charmed and sharp and kind and musical and crisp and crafty and unsorry and base and elegant".

Always an outsider, Geoff was, as Kirsten McDougall noted in her tribute, widely ignored by the official givers-out of grants and prizes and invitations to festivals. Until quite late in the day, that is, when he received the Janet Frame

11

Prize for Poetry in 2009, the inaugural Nigel Cox Award in 2010, and an Arts Foundation of New Zealand Te Tumu Toi Laureate Award in 2014. These meant a lot to him – although he met each occasion with his usual sardonic reserve, so you might not have known. I remember at the Arts Foundation's glitzy event the photographer marshalling Geoff and the other laureates. "Well I guess I'd better take my hat off then," he said. "No! Leave it on!" said the photographer.

Fergus Barrowman
1 September 2023

*Thanks to everybody who contributed, knowingly or unknowingly, to this selection, especially Pip Adam, Susanna Andrew, Jenny Bornholdt, James Brown, Paula Green, Anne Kennedy, Elizabeth Knox, Bill Manhire, Kirsten McDougall, Greg O'Brien, Carl Shuker, Damien Wilkins and Ashleigh Young, but the choices are mine.*

# INTERVIEW

*(Sport* 31, *2003)*

I interviewed Geoff Cochrane in August this year at his Berhampore flat, where he lives alone. It's a small one-bedroom place in a block of flats set a few metres back from a busy road. The traffic lets up at around 4am. Geoff moved here "for a weekend" – that was about ten years ago.

We sat in his living room which is also where he has his bed. He uses the other room for his writing room because the walls are too thin to allow him to sleep well in there. He works on an electronic typewriter – a source of some anguish to his publishers. A computer was trialled once and rejected – a gesture completely in keeping with his work, which can be both stubbornly austere and wonderfully witty.

Beside his chair there is a copy of T.S. Eliot's *Four Quartets*, and Canadian poet Anne Carson's *Men in the Off Hours*, borrowed from the public library. I ask him how he likes the Carson and he has an instant quote from it: "'Penguins topple like astonished dice.'" Geoff grins at me. "And you think, do they? And then you think, of course they do! That's real writing."

He smokes roll-your-owns throughout the interview, spreading a piece of newspaper on his lap to catch the spilled tobacco.

The clipped stylishness of his writing is also evident in his talk. He speaks in full sentences and with such care that you sometimes think he's reading from something. What he's reading from is, of course, his own mind – a place you feel he's lived in to an extent that makes our own mental habitations begin to seem transient, a bit half-hearted. Another way of putting it might be to observe that Geoff owns his ideas while we only seem to rent ours. His conversation has the range of a voracious reader and the depth of some voracious living. He is a provocative commentator on both activities.

Still, perhaps his most arresting statements come when he is considering writing, its folly and its power. It's difficult to think of another New Zealand writer who could formulate the following notion: "Whatever one writes is conditional. And it's probably sweeter and more replete for being conditional – is it not?" The Cochrane tone is one of the great pleasures in our literature – and somehow sweeter (to borrow his word) for appearing not to be part of that literature.

Despite his own misgivings when we took a break in recording ("You don't think I'm being too guarded, do you?"), what is striking about this interview is Geoff's generosity in the face of some fairly objectionable questioning. At times the interviewer seems to presume an intimacy ("How's your sex life, Geoff?"). Actually, though we've met several times over the last few years at bookish things, we've never spoken together for more than a few minutes.

My only defence is that my interest and intense admiration for Geoff's work made me think that everyone would be gripped by such inquiries – or at least by the responses they would draw. I still believe that. And I don't care to hide the evangelical push behind the appearance of this interview in print. Geoff Cochrane's continuing obscurity as a writer may appear as a "mystery" to the man himself; to those of us who've read him, it's something like a cruel and stupid joke.

My other defence for prying is that I love a good story and Geoff's full of them.

DAMIEN WILKINS

Your work is studded with references to writing as a profession, as a life choice, and these references carry a fair weight of self-deprecation or ambivalence. The central character in *Tin*

*Nimbus*, your first novel, says that "all writers are fools, their choice of profession proves that". And in *Blood*, your second novel, there's this observation: "The decision to write is formed of an acrid pall, the smoke from the ruins of manlier aspirations."

Can we start by talking about how you see the business of "being a writer" – was it a choice for you? Were there "manlier aspirations"?

### Geoff Cochrane

Absolutely. I was always going to be an artist of one sort or another. As a kid I painted and I drew and I acted and I sang. And I've always regarded writing as being an extension of the activities of painting and drawing. You use implements, you arrange words into various shapes on the page. But this business of feeling a kind of difference or inferiority because one is an artist in this community is inculcated into us fairly early. My father was a frustrated painter.

### Damien Wilkins

What was his job?

### Geoff Cochrane

He joined the TAB in 1952 when it was inaugurated. But earlier than that, when the war broke out, he served overseas in the Solomon Islands and so on and when he came back and tried to resume his draftsmanship and become a commercial artist, he found he was a man among boys really and his ambition withered.

Men of his generation took a very black and white view of their responsibilities as men. When Peter McIntyre, who'd been a war artist, made the decision when he came back from the war that he was going to turn himself into a professional painter, his decision was regarded as being frivolous – which I find very interesting. And I have always felt myself that in a sense art as an activity, writing as an activity, is somewhat frivolous. I mean there are more adult things one can be doing. I was six weeks into the writing of *Tin Nimbus* when it struck me like a thunderbolt that there really are few activities as essentially un-adult as writing a novel – this extended fiction that as the writer you have to inhabit for however many months it takes you.

### DAMIEN WILKINS

So why do it? Why not stop at the point you have that insight?

### GEOFF COCHRANE

Well, because it's fun. It's a complicated sort of fun, isn't it. And work, in inverted commas, is such a horrible, horrendous thing to have to do. And so I stop writing and I do precisely what? What is it that the world requires of me? Does the world really need yet another 52-year-old 10-stone builder's labourer?

### DAMIEN WILKINS

Which brings us to something I wanted to ask you about. In that passage I quoted from *Blood*, Abel Blood goes on to say: "I really want to refuse to eat or work, to deny the world my slightest collaboration, to let the years expend themselves while I swig my life away in some dim bar."

### GEOFF COCHRANE

It's very good, isn't it?

### DAMIEN WILKINS

Yes it is. So this spirit of refusal is behind the desire to write?

## GEOFF COCHRANE

Writing is certainly, for my part, an expression of my somewhat contrary nature. But the passage you cite, I glimpse in that the tail end of the comet of depression and unhappiness that was really my lot until I wrote a couple of novels.

## DAMIEN WILKINS

Well the tail end of that quote is of course drinking and that brings us to, I guess, what looks like, from the outside at least, the central fact of your life – your alcoholism. These days we'd tend to talk about a genetic predisposition towards addiction but are you suggesting that there was a philosophical component to the drinking? I wonder if you could take us back to that life: Wellington in the 70s. What was it like? The novels seem to suggest a scene, certain rules of conduct, a special lingo even. But I'm aware in asking that question that I'm treating *Blood*, say, as a documentary work – is it?

## GEOFF COCHRANE

The difficulty I had with writing both *Tin Nimbus* and *Blood* was that if I told the truth about my own experiences, I wouldn't be believed. Had I written an autobiography, people would have said he's made this up and he hasn't done a very good job either! He can't really expect us to swallow this.

I seemed to lead a sort of negative version of the charmed life. Things happened to me.

But alcoholism results from the convergence of all sorts of factors, and you're asking me really to what extent I consented. Now Dylan Thomas, when he was a boy of nine, said something interesting in this context. He was asked what he wanted to be when he grew up. And he said "the drunkest man in the world". Now I understand that. I can understand how, surrounded by merry drunken uncles and plenty of drinking, as one is given an Irish Catholic background, one can look upon heavy drinking as being quite an engaging sort of occupation.

### DAMIEN WILKINS

What about this business of there being a drinking scene. As it appears in your fiction, this is not an isolated existence. This is actually a community, isn't it?

### GEOFF COCHRANE

Yes. Centred around the Duke of Edinburgh Hotel in Wellington.

### DAMIEN WILKINS

And using a kind of special language. At some point you feel those novels are behaving like fantastic versions of something because of the way people speak to each other. Is that how people spoke?

### GEOFF COCHRANE

One could go into the Duke of Edinburgh and see there a special stratum of society – there were a certain number of dropouts who worked as window-cleaners and postmen and they had degrees. There was a sense in which they were withholding their labour too – just like Abel . . . like Able-bodied Blood or whatever I called him. And the first thing I noticed about that bar was the way in which everyone spoke – in this special, quite cultured way, and you could learn to do it. You could learn to do it in a week. And if you flew from Wellington to Auckland and went into the Kiwi Hotel in Auckland, you made a remarkable discovery, which was that everyone in the Kiwi Hotel spoke in exactly the same way as the people you'd left behind in the Duke.

## DAMIEN WILKINS

This seems to chime with a certain romantic view of the educated drunk, but you're saying that this was what it was like.

## GEOFF COCHRANE

Oh indeed. We read *Under the Volcano* by Malcom Lowry, and there were those who made pilgrimages to Mexico to see the locales.

One did join a family. It was extraordinary. And I made friends in those years that I never lost. Of course you had to penetrate it a bit.

## DAMIEN WILKINS

You had to drink a lot?

## GEOFF COCHRANE

You had to put in a lot of time. You had to attend, you see. More or less religiously. And I like to claim that I spent the last three years of that pub's existence in it, you know. I would have slept there, had I been allowed to.

## DAMIEN WILKINS

Connecting up that point about language – the language of the pub – with your own literary language, where did your style come from? There's a stateliness, a courtliness almost to your writing.

## GEOFF COCHRANE

But the language in the novels is more or less artificial anyway.

## DAMIEN WILKINS

So where did that style come from?

## Geoff Cochrane

I guess I thought it was just a nice quality one might build into a novel.

## Damien Wilkins

And were there other Cochrane styles tried and discarded before this one stuck? I'd want to suggest that this quality of voice is in the poetry too. How did it evolve?

## Geoff Cochrane

I can't remember. I can think of models that I might have followed, consciously or otherwise, Thornton Wilder being one. Where everything about a work is more or less mannered. Of course I came in for a lot of criticism when the novels were published. If I got a lame-brained reviewer, they were sure to say, "These people don't talk like proper people." Well they were never meant to.

## Damien Wilkins

One of the interesting things about your work – poems and fiction – is that it regards the former drinking life as not really "former" at all but sharply present – so the spirit of renunciation we might expect from the "recovering" person is not really there. In its place there's this wonderful tenderness towards the people and places who were with you, and a humour too. Can you talk about the ongoingness of these concerns? I mean, there's no sense in which your work announces that "this was all terrible and now we're moving on".

## Geoff Cochrane

Oh it was far from terrible. The results of it were more or less cataclysmic. I've probably chosen too strong a word there but they were almost fatal for me as an organism. Now some would say, I guess, that my demise as an organism would have been neither here nor there in the scheme of things but a day dawned when it was something I had to reckon with really.

But maybe I'm taking the piss a little bit when I threaten my reading public with perhaps still contemplating the notion of taking another drink or six.

Of course it isn't ever over for an alcoholic. There have been blokes who have been fifteen years off the grog and have finally won the Nobel Prize and are now flying to Stockholm and decide to have a gin on the plane. And six weeks later they have lost everything.

### DAMIEN WILKINS
Here's a stanza from "Under the Volcano" (*Vanilla Wine*, 2003):

Not a drop of alcohol
in eleven years,
but still I dream
the same old shame,
the same old prideful shame.

"Prideful shame" is very good – you are proud, aren't you?

### GEOFF COCHRANE
Yes. I suppose it has to be remarked at this juncture that I was quite an engaging drunk. I was voluble, loquacious, even eloquent as a drinker. I mean I could pass out mid-sentence – and these were not simple sentences!

### DAMIEN WILKINS
Can I ask you about the final lines of "Zigzags" (*Acetylene*, VUP, 2001), which is one of your most insistent poems about

"that time" – and probably quite atypical in its declamatory style. Here are the lines:

> Because I was a poet people died
> Because I was a poet, people died

Is this the "old shame" part of the remembering?

### GEOFF COCHRANE

Well, firstly, I wanted something to fall back on in readings. One discovers, usually at the last minute, that one hasn't got anything that lends itself to being read aloud. So "Zigzags" means I've got something. But I wrote that particular couplet at the risk of being misunderstood because it sounds like quite a self-indulgent sentiment, doesn't it. Actually it's merely a statement of fact. As a generation we really were prone to death by automobile and suicide and drug overdose and so on, and a lot of the friends of my twenties did in fact die.

### DAMIEN WILKINS

What's the connection though between that fact and you being a poet? On one reading you're casting yourself as a watcher of these events?

### GEOFF COCHRANE

Yes. No. Yes. But there seems to be more to it than I can explain, doesn't there?

### DAMIEN WILKINS

Your own death of course has also been rehearsed, hasn't it. Your new collection of poetry, *Vanilla Wine*, refers to this moment, and it opens a recent short story, "The Tenant": "I died in 1986 at the age of thirty-five." What happened and how did it affect things?

## Geoff Cochrane

I'm an asthmatic. And as an alcoholic my asthma was never properly controlled. In 1986 I developed a massive neuropathy of the legs. No one saw me during the course of 1986 because I was away in a bin learning to walk again. All this thanks to my drinking. The year 1986 was characterised by at least four very serious asthma attacks, the last two of which killed me, in a clinical sense. I had to be resuscitated, intubated, where they put tubes down into your lungs and they inflate your lungs artificially, and they also paralyse you with a thing called curare. So waking up to find oneself totally paralysed with one's lungs full of tubes is an interesting experience.

For years I carried around a sealed envelope given to me by a doctor, which for some extraordinary reason I never opened. And when I did open it I discovered I'd been meant to give it to my GP. It was a letter from this bloke who'd brought me back from the dead and it described my condition upon admission to Wellington Public Hospital. I found it interesting enough to write a poem about it, and then I was plagiarising myself when I used it again in that story – that's allowed once or twice in a career, isn't it?

## Damien Wilkins

That's allowed. While we're on the topic of mortality, the Australian writer Gerard Windsor wrote an essay about his own work in which he expresses concern, rather wittily but also in earnest, that one of his books doesn't have enough deaths in it. He says that "Looking hard and square at death is, I know, a criterion for me of serious literary worth. I am impatient with writing that doesn't run to intimations of mortality." And I thought about this in regard to your own work. Is there some sense in which you need a death or two in the book to somehow make the book?

## GEOFF COCHRANE

Oh absolutely. Surely sitting down to write a novel for instance, you're going for broke. My experience of writing novels is that one has to throw every fucking thing one has at them in order to make them stand up at all. There's a sense in which death is one of those available phenomena, like sex and romantic love and so on.

## DAMIEN WILKINS

Is it any wider than that though for you? More than just an option?

## GEOFF COCHRANE

Well, I'm a broken-down drunk and a lapsed Catholic. I have been going to funerals since I was knee-high to a grasshopper. Growing up in the Fifties in an extended Irish Catholic how's-your-father really acquaints one with death at a very early age. And then as I say, people kept dying on me.

## DAMIEN WILKINS

I recall you saying once that you regarded being born in New Zealand as something of a disaster for you.

## GEOFF COCHRANE

An unqualified disaster.

## DAMIEN WILKINS

An unqualified disaster. On that occasion you were talking about some earlier ambitions to write thrillers, and New Zealand couldn't supply the right goods for the genre.

## GEOFF COCHRANE

As a young bloke one conceived of writing a little thriller or murder mystery. But no, you couldn't, the names of the streets and so on were all wrong, Pigeon Park just didn't have the same ring as Piccadilly Circus.

One had no hope of becoming a film director, either. Why? Because one was saddled with living in a backwater. One hails from Island Bay or fucking Miramar. I mean, when Geoff Murphy and Bruno Lawrence were making *The Tank Busters*, they had to build their own fucking crane – which they made out of wood!

That was something I had to face at the age of eighteen. I was a fairly talented young guy. And I could have gone several ways. But as I said, the possibility of, say, becoming a film director, you know . . .

### DAMIEN WILKINS
But people did though, didn't they.

### GEOFF COCHRANE
Oh not until years later. I mean you had people claiming to be film directors who made documentaries for the National Film Unit. That was your only option.

### DAMIEN WILKINS
The other option of course was to leave the country. Have you travelled?

### GEOFF COCHRANE
No, I never achieved exit velocity. And my twenty years of drinking was responsible for that. I knew in my twenties that if I got as far as Sydney, I'd never see New Zealand again – that amounted to a conviction. Actually England would have been the place for me. God knows what would have become of me.

I never did feel rooted in New Zealand. That changes as you get older.

## DAMIEN WILKINS

That's really interesting because when I was reading through your poetry, I became aware of an absence, and it was this: there is none of that staple of NZ poetry books, the poem from overseas, looking back. So there's no "over there" stuff and now you're saying you never felt you belonged here either.

## GEOFF COCHRANE

Well, my trick nowadays is just to say that I'm an international poet. Seriously. And you yourself have set a bit of an example in this regard, for which I see you're criticised by some wanker in a recent *Listener*, by writing, by pretending to be an American fiction writer, and why not! Why not if it gets the book written.

## DAMIEN WILKINS

And if it's a good book, isn't that it?

## GEOFF COCHRANE

Indeed.

## DAMIEN WILKINS

Just staying on this topic. For most New Zealand writers – and particularly poets – there's usually an orientation one can pick out – some leaning towards or away from certain key figures in NZ lit: Baxter maybe, Curnow, Manhire – but I'm not sure in your case whether this sort of mapping makes sense. Were you aware of other New Zealand poets when you started writing? Did you write "against" anybody, or were there meaningful affinities?

## GEOFF COCHRANE

Not really. I had found myself constitutionally incapable of taking New Zealand literature seriously. But this is a generational thing. I belong to a generation that eschewed its own product pretty much. To this day, I meet blokes of my own age who are otherwise quite literate people but who will not, on principle, read a novel by a New Zealander. They simply never get round to it. And I'm ashamed to confess to this but I'm a wee bit like that myself.

In any case, when I began to write verse, you had your monuments, your Curnows, Masons, Fairburns, Baxters and your Glovers, and then you had the rest of them, and poets were a dime a dozen – you discovered this to your dismay. They really were a dime a dozen and one really didn't distinguish himself from the next. And perhaps I took the somewhat lofty view that I was almost certain to be better than most of them anyway!

Certainly I took Baxter pretty seriously. I could see of course that Baxter was a very derivative writer but that didn't prevent him assuming quite some stature – even in my book. You had only to spend five minutes in his company to know that you'd really met someone who mattered. I was lucky enough to meet him on a couple of occasions and he made a fucking impression. By that time he was writing the wonderful *Jerusalem Sonnets*, and I remember buying the little chapbook called *The Junkies & the Fuzz*, and here he was addressing a live contemporary issue.

I was always a little troubled by Curnow's syntax but I liked him.

### Damien Wilkins

Did you go to university?

### Geoff Cochrane

No. By the time I'd left college I'd had enough. My last year at college was a complete and absolute disaster – a disaster from which I'm really still recovering. No wonder I drank.

## Damien Wilkins

What happened?

## Geoff Cochrane

Well it was the extent of my failure which really I now see resulted from a sort of nervous breakdown, which nowadays would be recognised and dealt with but they did absolutely none of that in those days and I was allowed to leave college, and quite a good college it was too, with nothing.

## Damien Wilkins

You mean you didn't sit the exams?

## Geoff Cochrane

Oh it's too complicated to go into but I was already a man among boys.

I was constantly being told I was lazy. It was something I never believed entirely. I think this relates to the alcoholism, this humiliation I experienced as a young man. Auden says somewhere and I didn't read this until years later – that art is born of humiliation.

## Damien Wilkins

There's your poem, "The Poet", in which you talk of this, about life being a convalescence: "a slow, elated, awed recovery/ from humiliation." Let's move forward to publishing. Through the late Seventies and Eighties, you started publishing your poems in small editions, where the publication was arranged by friends. How did that work exactly?

## Geoff Cochrane

Stephen Murphy was my first publisher. I was living under his roof, I think. And for once in my sad life I actually had access to a typewriter. So I sat down and typed up some poems I'd been carrying around in manuscript – or did some gorgeous blonde do this for me? I can't quite remember! Anyway, Murphy was a great host and these poems were passed around. And Stephen, who had a bit of money – he was studying law – said haughtily, "Damn it, I'll publish!" And so in the fullness of time that first little volume appeared. It was largely a question of singing for one's supper, you know.

## Damien Wilkins

Had you been sending stuff to magazines?

## Geoff Cochrane

Well I remember being published by Sam Hunt in something, and Rhys Pasley included a piece of mine in *Lipsync* – could I have been as young as eighteen or nineteen?

I guess I've always been one to do things my way and publishing those little private press books was always a bit of a way of cocking a snook at those people who produced literary magazines. I mean who in Christ's name reads literary magazines?

## Damien Wilkins

In 1992, VUP published *Aztec Noon*, which selected poems from those early books as well as a bunch of new poems. This was your first mainstream book – did publication make you feel that you'd "arrived" – was it momentous or did you think, "what took them so long?"

## Geoff Cochrane

I had my last drink in 1989, in a bar in Island Bay. And I went through the Salvation Army Bridge Programme, which would be as good as any alcohol treatment programme you'll find in the world. And the thing they teach you is to set goals for yourself. So one thing I thought to myself I must absolutely do and as soon as possible is to publish a book of verse with a proper publisher. And I hadn't been sober very long when a mate of mine, Lindsay Rabbitt, said to me, "You're coming to the launch of such-and-such a book at Unity Books and I'm going to introduce you to Fergus Barrowman." Well, that meeting with Fergus Barrowman changed my life really. Because had certain tiles not fallen into place within two or three years of my getting sober then I don't like to think what would have happened to me. I certainly had the feeling that the machinery had started to tick over for me when Fergus accepted the manuscript of that book of verse which I think he did within a fortnight of meeting me. He's a wee bit slower these days.

### Damien Wilkins

It was seven years until your second "major collection" as it says on the back of the book, came out, *Into India*. In that time you were busy writing novels. Was this the long-held desire for fiction finally working itself out? Were there stories lying about? What was the process?

### Geoff Cochrane

I began writing by writing fiction.

### Damien Wilkins

But you were known as a poet.

### Geoff Cochrane

It's a damn sight easier to be a poet than to be a fiction writer.

### Damien Wilkins

The hours, you mean? The sweat, the labour, the imagining a world?

## Geoff Cochrane

Well, Sam Hunt says this. You know, he was asked, "Why verse, Sam?" "Because it's shorter."

## Damien Wilkins

But was writing a novel one of these goals you set yourself?

## Geoff Cochrane

Absolutely, yes. I'd said to myself I was going to sit down and have a serious attempt at a novel. Forget for a moment this nancy notion of writing poems and, you know, do the hard work. My attitude was, at that stage of the game, that you really weren't a fully adult writer, a legitimate writer, until you'd written at least one novel.

## Damien Wilkins

The reception to *Tin Nimbus* set a sort of pattern: overwhelmingly positive reviews – real raves – and a shortlisting for the Commonwealth Prize – and hardly any sales. That was 1995. Two years later, *Blood* came out. Again the people that read it loved it, but again disappointing sales. How did this affect you as a writer?

## Geoff Cochrane

It didn't affect me as a writer but it certainly affected me as a man – it grew me up. You can imagine the sort of unhappinesses that experiences like those engender but you simply have to get over that – or perish. You do that as a man rather than as a writer.

I like to think, you know, that I regard my literary fortunes with a good deal more equanimity than a younger writer could bring to the task.

## DAMIEN WILKINS

You wrote other novels after this – which remain unpublished. This is an odd thing to happen to a writer – odd being a rather mild and inadequate word.

## GEOFF COCHRANE

Yes but they're odd novels.

## DAMIEN WILKINS

The usual pattern is the writer who begins with the unpublished novels and then graduates to a kind of perpetuity of publishing. What do you think of those lost novels? Are they lost?

## GEOFF COCHRANE

I guess my attitude to them is that they're like the unborn child, you know. They're the abortions really, whatever qualities they might have or lack.

One of them, *Jungle Altars*, is deliberately formless. A rush of blood to the head and I thought, I'll make my third novel which is bound to be published now I belong to a wonderful publishing house, I'll make it as formless as hell and with my knack of introducing symmetry within the last few pages, I'll pull it all together at the last minute and it'll be fucking wonderful. Well, I doubt that it is. And I guess there's a lesson here that you abandon your received rules and even those of your own invention at your peril.

I mean the last thing a publisher wants really, and I'm not directing this at VUP, but the last thing a publisher wants is originality. What he wants is a book that resembles another book. They've got enough headaches and enough on their plates without having to nut out ways of selling something like *Jungle Altars*.

## Damien Wilkins

Can I just return you to an earlier point you made about having this problem, this lack of faith or belief in New Zealand literature – once you became a "mainstream" author, having your work reviewed, appearing in readings and so on, did that attitude change? Do you feel you're part of something now?

## Geoff Cochrane

I don't feel I've yet become a mainstream author. To return to a point you made earlier, people who read me like me. I would have a 98 per cent hit rate on that score. But people won't read me. And it's a mystery to me. And it probably remains a mystery to my publisher.

I sense a resistance in the media to my name. There is a curious impermeability there surrounding certain organs.

## Damien Wilkins

Is that to do with what you've called the "unfashionable" things you write about? That somehow alcoholism and that life is not deemed worthy of attention?

## Geoff Cochrane

Well, there's that but I think that's a different argument. I'm talking about the media and it seems to me that the only way to be known to the people who make arts programmes on TV is to be known already.

But you were asking about belonging to a thing called New Zealand literature, and the truth is you can have books published and you can be asked to do the odd reading and still not meet . . . well, I mean I meet you and I meet James Brown and I meet Greg O'Brien and Jenny Bornholdt. But one never meets Maurice Gee, for instance. One never meets Janet Frame. One never meets . . . I mean the list is endless of the people one never meets.

I remember thinking that when I was first published by VUP that a wonderful literary friendship was going to come of this. But it hasn't happened. I still don't have to write to anyone. My afternoons, thank God, are my own. I don't have to write to any bastard!

### Damien Wilkins

Last year, you reverted to type or something, and put out a slim volume of fiction, *Brindle Embers*, through your friend Gerald Melling. This is already a cult book – the cult is made up of other writers mainly – I know Greg O'Brien and Barbara Anderson are big fans of the book. It contains some remarkable pieces. What pushed you towards the short form?

### Geoff Cochrane

I just love it. Look, because no one gives a fuck whether I live or die as a writer, I can do what I like pretty much. I woke up to this fact and it was like a liberation.

You can write a short story, a good one, in a week. And you can finish it in exactly the same spirit as you started it. Consider this: there you are, slaving away on your novel and long before you've finished it, your poor fucking novel has died and gone to novel heaven. There's so much willing involved in writing a novel. All this business of getting people in and out of taxis! You can dispense with that in writing a short story.

### Damien Wilkins

Where do you see those pieces of short fiction fitting in your work?

### GEOFF COCHRANE

I think, as exercises in style, they are among the best things I've ever written.

### DAMIEN WILKINS

I'd agree.

### GEOFF COCHRANE

That's terrific then. And the next lot, they're even better.

### DAMIEN WILKINS

So that's what you're working on now?

### GEOFF COCHRANE

Oh yes, there's another lot on the way.

### DAMIEN WILKINS

And what will you do with those in terms of publishing?

### GEOFF COCHRANE

Well, Gerald Melling likes publishing little books and so he's going to do them. And maybe downstream someone will hopefully collect them.

### DAMIEN WILKINS

I'd like to talk about the poetry now, though there are strong connections between the fiction and the poems. What your work offers are several terrific self-descriptions, I guess – I mean of your own aesthetics. Here is one of my favourites, from "Postcard" (*Aztec Noon*, 1992):

> I try to craft a thing as big
> as a matchbox, as explicit.

There are several things to take from such an image – a matchbox is a rather beautiful invention, isn't it? A form perfectly suited to its function but it also has a concealed part. I'd like to ask about that word "explicit" – what does that mean for you in terms of the way your poems offer up their meanings? I guess I don't think of you as a very difficult poet.

## GEOFF COCHRANE

No. It's one of my aims – perhaps it's the frustrated copywriter in me – but I do believe you're in the business of communicating. And you had better well bloody hook the reader with the first line and take him at least as far as the end of the first stanza. In my view, if you're not doing that, if you're not consciously attempting to do that, then you're misguided.

## DAMIEN WILKINS

But how do you stop the poem becoming too available? When a poem becomes "obvious" does it stop being interesting?

## GEOFF COCHRANE

Oh Christ all that, yes. There's nothing very new in any of this. Transparency and so on. In my day we were reading the incredibly obscure densities of Dylan Thomas and pretending it was all wonderful but really . . . I mean, you didn't have to read too far into it to know that you'd rather be reading something that did at least offer you a meaning that was, you know, graspable first time round. A poem shouldn't necessarily yield all its meaning first time round but there again I can't see any reason why it shouldn't.

## DAMIEN WILKINS

Here's another sort of mission statement:

I write in order to have
degrees of clarity –
if not solutions, legible diagrams.
("Rads", *Acetylene*, 2001)

"Legible diagrams" is lovely, and though it's not quite what these lines intend, it makes me think of someone tracing your walking route around the city, Wellington – the kind of physical movement that's often there in the poems. You walk every day, don't you?

### GEOFF COCHRANE

Absolutely. When I think about the act of walking, and it gets my endorphins going, and it keeps me fit – well fit enough to do all that walking – I think of Joyce and what he had to say about walking around Dublin. Most of the time it's just white noise. What's going on in your head is just nonsense really. But every once in a while the noise might clear and you might get a line or two, an image, something.

### DAMIEN WILKINS

What's the pattern of your day then?

### GEOFF COCHRANE

I rise early. I don't sleep much these days – particularly if I know there's an interviewer imminent. I listen to the news on the National Programme, and then when I get pissed off with that, I begin to write. I have the luxury, I'm single, I don't have anyone I have to respond to, so I can pretty much please myself. When I was working on the novels I was making myself work for at least three hours a day. But writing short stories and poems, you have the luxury of saying, well I've done enough now – particularly if you have.

I have to say that as a life, I wouldn't swap it for anything.

It's a wonderful wonderful life.

And then I have this wonderful walk into town.

### DAMIEN WILKINS

Is it the walking that makes you a poet of the weather? There's a lot of light and wind and sky and rain stuff in the poems . . .

### GEOFF COCHRANE

I like to think of myself as the pre-eminent Wellington poet but no one else has noticed it so far.

### DAMIEN WILKINS

We should have a ceremony to announce it.

### GEOFF COCHRANE

I should be inaugurated, yes.

### DAMIEN WILKINS

One thing that interests me about your work is this remarkable search always for the new word, the new conjunction, I suppose, to get at the effects of light on surfaces:

Deliquescent clouds decoct
the stink of solder and flux. The light
could be said to falter.
("Noon", *Aztec Noon*, VUP, 1992)

This is not an everyday vocabulary, is it? It's not even your average poet's vocabulary, is it?

### GEOFF COCHRANE

Well most poets are scientific illiterates. Why they should be is beyond me. "Deliquescent" is a word with scientific connotations. Interestingly enough, most people misuse the word "deliquescent", to mean the opposite of deliquescent.

Something else going on, if we're thinking about language, is the inheritance of church liturgy. There's the wonderful couplet:

> Sufficient unto the day
> are the two-minute noodles thereof.
> ("Bunker Bulletins", *Vanilla Wine*, 2003)

That's the parodic side of it, but clearly Catholicism has left its residue – can you talk about this? Is this primarily linguistic or is that too narrow? Is there a world-view that still hangs around?

Geoff Cochrane
You never get over it. God knows it put us through the hoops, didn't it?

Damien Wilkins
Well I never had a Catholic education.

Geoff Cochrane
Oh, a Catholic education was the pits. I remember reading *Portrait of the Artist as a Young Man* at the age of eighteen and I thought, Christ, this was written fifty or sixty years ago and he could be describing St Pat's College (Town).

Damien Wilkins
I remember reading that and thinking this is a real period piece.

## GEOFF COCHRANE

I have younger siblings brought up by Catholic teachers who had an entirely different experience to mine.

Catholicism is a huge subject. It's a bit like escaping from Stalinist Russia, I guess. In this respect Koestler made this very observation. He said you find your way into communism via a few deceptively simple syllogisms and the next thing you know you're inside a sphere where the walls are made of one syllogism connected to another, and there's no way out of it.

My way out of it was that the doubts began when I was about twelve or thirteen and then came to a sort of head at the age of sixteen, by which time the battle was a largely intellectual one. And I couldn't find my way out of the sphere, until I read a little essay by Bertrand Russell called "Why I Am Not a Christian". In that essay he describes himself at the age I then was, himself inside this sphere and he said that late one night he made the breakthrough. He said that if it was logical to posit a cause without a cause, then it was just as logical to posit a universe without a cause. And that was the intellectual breakthrough that allowed Russell to break from Christianity and allowed me to break from Catholicism.

But one retains a certain respect for the church.

## DAMIEN WILKINS

You wrote an essay for Mark Williams' anthology of NZ writers on Catholicism, *The Source of the Song*.

## GEOFF COCHRANE

It's a nostalgia really. You grow up believing that all your rewards will come in a posthumous existence, that justice will be done in a posthumous existence. If I lost my faith at the age of eighteen, it wasn't until years later that I came to appreciate how much I'd lost.

40

## Damien Wilkins

That comes across in the essay. And there you quote your own novel *Blood* about your time as an altar boy. You're trying to get at the heart of the appeal of the church ritual, the consecration of the Eucharist: "it had the purity of an equation, the gaunt persuasiveness of a basic sum" – which might be a sort of description of your own style.

## Geoff Cochrane

I don't know if I'm in a position to comment. I like what I wrote. You know, you write these things then you forget about them.

## Damien Wilkins

In a few of these questions we've been skirting that awkward term "confessional". And it seems right now to move from the Church to the confessional, doesn't it? Robert Lowell features a few times in poems, he's name-checked. What do you think of the term "confessional": is it useful to you? I guess confessional poetry has a stigma attached to it, doesn't it?

## Geoff Cochrane

Well, in New Zealand, you couldn't realistically set out to be a confessional writer of any sort without being likely to end up on the front page of *Truth*. It's too small a community to this day to allow you the freedom of indiscretion.

## Damien Wilkins

But aren't you confessional in terms of holding up your own life for inspection?

## Geoff Cochrane

Well, I'm holding up a semblance of my life for inspection. There are things I choose not to discuss or touch upon.

I remember saying to myself I would make a wonderful confessional writer but I lack the courage – or, more accurately, my family lacks the courage. When I was writing *Tin Nimbus* I had to believe it was going to be published and therefore this was going to be the book that would be posted home to Levin, for the parents to read. Had I been living in New York and my parents living in fucking Milwaukee, I might have had an excuse for not posting it home.

### Damien Wilkins

Of course above this issue, we should hang this line, which is one of the funniest lines in confessional poetry: "I'm diagnosed as having . . . never mind." ("Milestones", *Acetylene*, 2001) Does the confessor get sick of his own sins?

### Geoff Cochrane

I guess.

### Damien Wilkins

I mean that line is a joke, isn't it, against the form.

### Geoff Cochrane

Is that allowed? From time to time, one gets antsy about one's work. Occasionally I have a look through *Jungle Altars*, one of my unpublished novels, and I think there's too much sex in it, by half. So there are questions of bourgeois taste here, aren't there.

### Damien Wilkins

I want to come back to sex.

### Geoff Cochrane

Oh good. But listen, I wanted to say this, to someone or to a tape recorder. You hit fifty and it all hoves into view. Food

42

and sex really become less important somehow, and you find yourself taking a more cerebral pleasure in things. I can sit here watching the most mindless thing on TV and it delights me. But it delights me on a sort of intellectual level. Does this make any sense to you?

DAMIEN WILKINS

A little.

GEOFF COCHRANE

Well, it'll come. You're a good ten years younger than me.

DAMIEN WILKINS

In *Acetylene* you include poems which are titled "Worksheets", and these appear to be entries from a writing journal, notes to yourself, fragments – and I was interested in why you'd include these.

GEOFF COCHRANE

It relates to a technical difficulty I had which is that I'm fond of writing the short poem, the poem with only a couple of lines. But there's a limit to the number of poems of only a couple of lines that you can put in a book, and so I just designed a little container.

DAMIEN WILKINS

So these aren't your worksheets, these are very carefully crafted documents?

GEOFF COCHRANE

Yes but they're supposed to partake of the disorder that a real worksheet might.

## Damien Wilkins

I'd like to quote from "This Morning's Viewpoint" (*Acetylene*, 2001), which tells the story of an interrupted romance, a botched love affair:

> My purpose was to kiss her.
> You'd think a man of my age
> Might have pulled *that* off.

Then the last line is: "Misery is contemptible." Probably I should be cautioned by that title – that this is a viewpoint held for a morning – and yet I want to make more of it. This is a kind of creed, isn't it, for you? The poems and the fiction might live in reduced circumstances but their tone is never despairing?

## Geoff Cochrane

No. The tone of the work is never despairing but perhaps one senses that the man might be.

It's a thing I've come to realise as I've gotten older that really I am saved in a lot of situations by my sense of humour. And I think I'm a far more ironical writer than I'm sometimes given credit for.

## Damien Wilkins

Can I ask about the sequence you wrote on the death of your father, which is called "Whispers" – for many Cochrane-watchers this is one of your best. It's not simply candour we're admiring here. For me the heart-breaking details of the squeaky polystyrene coffee cups and the priest eating an ice-cream in the cinema complex – these bring the whole situation into focus. Can you talk about this poem?

My father was a long time dying. And I'm dismayed when I see the recent bill – the right-to-die bill – defeated by a lot of complacent politicians. Because in spite of all the talk we hear from clinicians about their wonderful ability to alleviate pain and how no one need die in pain, my father died in agony – and dementia.

I was commuting from Wellington to Levin on a weekly basis over a period of months. And I remember writing an entry in my diary at the time, "My father is dying and it's like watching paint dry." And I knew I couldn't put that in a poem.

Anyway, I had plenty of time to look at the things that were going on around us at the time, stuff that distracted us, I guess. There was a lot of stuff I couldn't put into the poem. Like the elderly dementia patient who used to sit on the veranda not far from my father's bedroom and talk to me in the most intriguing schizophrenese. I mean if you paid a surrealist poet they couldn't come up with this sort of word porridge . . . it was delightful.

It was an easy poem to write and it's always a bit astonishing to be told that what you found easy to write is liked more than things which took a long time and were harder. I had little to do but be there.

On the night he died, I'd wanted to go home at about 11.30pm but my youngest brother, who'd recently qualified as a general nurse, pulled into the carpark and I was prevailed upon to stay for another hour. So finally there were five of us in the room and my brother Phillip was monitoring Dad's pulse and at around one in the morning Phillip said, "He's arrested." Just like that. As matter-of-fact as that. Because he had his fingers on his wrist. And we all sat up and took notice. Had I been left alone in the room with him after all those weeks and months of watching his suffering, I would have missed the moment at which he actually died. I would have missed it.

DAMIEN WILKINS

Your family have read the poem?

GEOFF COCHRANE

Presumably. You never know what people read and what they don't.

DAMIEN WILKINS

But you felt no compunction about publishing.

GEOFF COCHRANE

I've kind of gotten over this. I think on the eve of the publication of *Blood*, had I been able to stop it, I would have. Greg McGee said the same thing about *Foreskin's Lament*, had he been able to stop it, he would have done so. I think by the time that poem about my father appeared, I'd toughened myself up a bit.

DAMIEN WILKINS

To return to the Catholic essay there's something else I'd like to pick up on as a way into talking about sexuality, which is pretty central to your work, isn't it?

GEOFF COCHRANE

Well, sex is, yes.

DAMIEN WILKINS

Sex, okay. In that essay you write that "I seem to myself to have been always sexually aware and active as a child". And this observation comes immediately after you've quoted a piece of Joyce's *Portrait of the Artist as a Young Man*, which

46

depicts hell as millions of rotting, stinking corpses. It's a vivid and troubling conjunction – what did you mean by it, and what did you mean by the sexually active child?

## Geoff Cochrane

When I read Freud I took issue with what he calls the latency period. I couldn't remember a time when I wasn't sexually aware, when I didn't have sexual feelings, and I couldn't, for that matter, remember a time when I wasn't at least trying to be sexually active.

Is it possible to reinforce the attractiveness of sex? If it is, the Catholic Church succeeds. Someone else made the observation long ago that Catholics make wonderful pornographers.

## Damien Wilkins

Just another of our great talents! But this does bring us to the adult sexuality of the novels.

## Geoff Cochrane

Kind of a contradiction in terms, I've always felt, adult sex.

## Damien Wilkins

Why?

## Geoff Cochrane

What could be less adult than sex? It appals me that we're so keen as a society about reserving unto ourselves the delights of sex. You will be eighteen or sixteen or whatever the age of consent is, and you will be married if at all possible. Capitalism does this to us, of course. Sex is the ultimate reward fed us by the capitalist machine.

Living alone as I do, to the extent that you never get any sex, you never get touched or kissed, which seems to me to be an extraordinary inversion of the pyramid, if you like. I mean it's easier to get sex – if you're prepared to pay for it – than it is to get physical affection.

### Damien Wilkins

I wanted to ask about the sex in *Blood*, which is a source of discomfort to some of your readers.

### Geoff Cochrane

Is it? Name them.

### Damien Wilkins

I'll supply a list later on. But Abel Blood has sex with Marika in the Hotel St George – and significantly, St Mary of the Angels church can be seen from the hotel room window. The Church again.

### Geoff Cochrane

I'm not a symbolist.

### Damien Wilkins

What I thought was that novel is really an argument for what – intimacy? At one point the narrator makes this plea on behalf of the era as against present aridities – "when did this fear of emotional attachment take hold". And that time he says was a time of "sexual amateurs": "We were democratic and game."

### Geoff Cochrane

Oh we were. And if my memory serves me correctly the women in the book are very sexually forward.

### Damien Wilkins

Is that book then a sort of act of nostalgia for a better time?

## GEOFF COCHRANE

Well, we had it all really. We did. We had it all. We had the liberation of women. Women could behave . . . they could be as randy as sailors. I mean it put an entire generation of men at a disadvantage really because we never learned how to seduce women – we didn't have to. Women came to us. All we had to do was wear our flared jeans and grow our hair long and the women came to us. I mean the sex I had in my twenties . . . I get none nowadays but, you know . . . it was on for one and all. And it made me like women a good deal more than I previously had.

## DAMIEN WILKINS

I wonder whether the readers who respond negatively to the book read it as a sort of male fantasy?

## GEOFF COCHRANE

Oh, no fantasy about it. Oh no no no. There was this sexual generosity at work. I mean everyone got some and it didn't seem to cause much misery.

## DAMIEN WILKINS

The intensity of the language around sex has another motor, doesn't it? Abel Blood is no longer a "player" in the "sexual zone", as he calls it: "The grim and the disappointed – those starved of life by life – they don't have a card, you see, their voices have the wrong timbre and won't do the trick." He talks about his own "bitter sexual isolation".

## GEOFF COCHRANE

Which if you are sexually isolated, you do experience this deep bitterness – in your forties, which I was when I wrote that book.

And later on, there's one of the most remarkable passages of "confessional prose" when he talks about the "risible error" of writing at such length: "the celibate have time on their hands"; "For at the most dry and candid level of myself, in my most sober but unflinching heart, I know I'm in a condition of retraction or withdrawal, a state which confers a bleak social abeyance." I'm risking a hopeless reductiveness here but does Abel's declaration capture at least one of your own moods? "Retraction"? "Withdrawal"? "Abeyance"?

GEOFF COCHRANE

I think it's fair to say that Geoff Cochrane was in that position in his forties. My situation now hasn't changed but I have changed. It matters less to me. Whether that's because I'm getting older and my hormones are not so clamorous any longer, I don't know. It's interesting to note that by the time a man is sixty, he has the blood testosterone level of a nine-year-old boy. You don't get this impression from watching television, do you?

DAMIEN WILKINS

So you'd rewrite that book now, or it would be a different book now?

GEOFF COCHRANE

That's always the way. Whatever one writes is conditional. And it's probably sweeter and more replete for being conditional – is it not?

DAMIEN WILKINS

Yes. And now you're the poet who "smiles at babies in supermarket aisles".

## GEOFF COCHRANE
Something of a comedown, yes.

## DAMIEN WILKINS
Does this mean you're getting happier?

## GEOFF COCHRANE
Look, I've got bad news for all those of my readers who are in their thirties and forties. It's almost inevitable that you will get happier.

At the age of eighteen, I thought, due to a constellation of circumstances I appeared to be at the centre of, that the only moral thing I could do would be to shoot myself or to throw myself under a train. I was in an intellectual cul-de-sac, driven by feelings of unutterable sadness really. I guess the point I want to make is that I can't conceive of being in that same situation ever again. I can conceive of myself being in the position of the Roman senator played by Charles Laughton in Stanley Kubrick's *Spartacus* who simply realises that his world is about to fall down around his ears and climbs into a tepid bath and slits his wrists – but that's another situation entirely.

## DAMIEN WILKINS
Let's end on the big note, the "what are we all here for" note . . . There's an interview with the American essayist Joseph Epstein in which he recalls a review written by Philip Larkin of one of Epstein's books of essays, and Larkin wondered who needed them, these essays of Epstein – "surely a case of supply rather than demand" – which is a great line, and also in its sourness dispenses a truth. Who needs these poems of Cochrane's? Who needs any writer's work? I wonder as a writer and a reader what it is you use literature for? Aesthetic bliss? Moral guidance? What?

Distraction. Though you get happier with the years, you less and less frequently experience anything resembling bliss.

Martin Amis talks somewhere of the various complicated pleasures we derive from reading. And the pleasures we derive from reading are akin to the pleasures we derive from writing, though for me . . . and I think the interview began somewhere in the vicinity of this assertion: I'm a maker of things. I was born to be a maker. If I wasn't a maker of poems and stories, I'd be a painter, and if I wasn't a painter, I'd be a maker of . . . letterboxes or something. There's a distinction in kind here between the intellectual and the artist, and I'm quite happy to be identified as belonging to the latter group.

There is an extent to which one has to fill one's time on earth with a more or less meaningful activity and I very much like what Kingsley Amis said and maybe we should let him have the last word. He said, there is no point to existence, but there is a point to art.

# Selected Poems

# AN AMBULANCE

Between hospital and zoo
asterisks of rain fall audibly
on the many old tin awnings.
Through cool blue air arrives
a siren's pure ambulance. Someone
is dying of too much afternoon,
of fennel and cats and clothes props.

## THE SHRIKE

*from "The Lament of Lao Tze"*

Jaundiced with lunar error
the sullen moon is menace
to any equanimity of thought
and makes of these liquor dregs
a bright undrinkable.

This mottled September sky
draws up in me a horror
like a rising mass of tepid blood.

I remember the frantic shrike
which drove in at our window
broken and mad with blindness.

My limpid, aquarian heart
is as cruel as water . . .

When did my wakefulness begin?

## "THE SETTLEMENT" / TWILIGHT

The tables are drenched – drenched, too,
with lilac petals
whose tiny saucers cup drops of rain.

Building night, cloud upon dirtier cloud
stack ruin above the harbour.

Under sodium-vapour streetlamps
a river smokes yellowly,
while cities grow, like crystals, on a moon

where we may meet in dreams.

## THE SEA THE LANDSMAN KNOWS

*for Rod Hall*

The sea the landsman knows, saltless and blue,
denies the death at its deep green bottom;

denies that dark heave of menace
you pilot your sleeping skipper through,

perched above a thumping marine V.8.,
your fingers the gimbals of a lodestone heart.

Shipping life, we founder,
but liquor makes us buoyant,

so here's to the faceless, mooning drowned
who dream forever of anchors and mermaids

where fish-shaped fish and shower-curtain seaweeds
bubble transparency skyward, and are never rained on.

## FOR BOB ORR, AGAIN

A week's absence – you'll choke;
I return to my room this morning
to find the only thing left
an immovable Underwood 'writer

I'd defy you to want to pinch.
They tell me I laugh in my sleep.
Well, I have a brother of whom I'm fond.
I dreamed him dead the other night,

as firm in death as apples.
Youth, beauty, Easter fucking Island;
that's the quality of dream you get nowadays,
laughter or not.

Construct instead a pyramid of strings,
an airy cage of lines, as merely lines
as maps or atlases, to sharpen razors in.
And live in it I reckon, Bob.

## POSTCARD

A sky the texture of peaches
mixes itself like paint.

I try to craft a thing as big
as a matchbox, as explicit.

Night snaps itself together.

Your visit is a postcard
from a distant, brilliant room
overlooking musical lawns.

I mark them down,
the things which once contained us;

the flower stall, flute and accordion,
the drizzle in which
we missed our departing selves.

## AZTEC NOON

This I had thought forgotten
I recall now almost perfectly
in the gloom of winter:

past a cloacal wall whose posters
decayed like leonine faces,
I took you home up steps,

strewn with crates and cabbage,
to a room which seemed a tank of light
at the very top of the world.

All summer was a gala Aztec noon
we walked in, hip to hip,
through odour of the sea's green cistern.

## NOON

In the dimness of noon
an upturned boat collects rain.

Deliquescent clouds decoct
the stink of solder and flux. The light
could be said to falter.

It is as if someone
dies by electrocution. Gulls scream
jubilence. They know the air is
cooling to a dimness

in which can be built oblivion.

## THE RETREAT

It all seemed flight, the early part.

At a sandy halt on the road away
from the place of our defeat,
all was air and light.

Men drank and bathed and were quiet.

For the present, mutton stewed,
a brown, cosmetic fume
hung in a stand of poplars some yards off

and we thought it Sunday.

## REPORT ON SOBRIETY

I write with my paper
between nib and rifle-butt.

Stinking of garlic cooking-oil and cats,
behind the house in which I doss
is a walled space like a cube
in which one might shoot
hostages, conjurers.

Sometimes, in drizzle, mice
nibble toxin-coloured lichen there.

I am the people I loathe, my past
appals me, me.

In films about rivers and fever
the smokes of war and those of the jungle
do the same pink swirling.

# INTO INDIA

Her solidity was rumoured.

I thought of her body
as something to travel to,
a goal hard of attainment.

Well, I'd make the journey.
I'd see this monument,
stone temple steeped in moonlight –

unless I found myself
in the neighbourhood beyond,
where dogs starve and chickens limp
and a man's corpse is hollow.

## TINAKORI NIGHTS

1

This is where cloud
disinvents light.
This is where the weather
conducts its slow experiments in dampness.
Near these hills took place
some wonderful parties, a suicide or two,
a few ardent fuckings.
She was skinny and brown,
a pallid T connecting hips and twat.

2

The hills breed climate, wetness.
At night they float a fine precipitation.
And these moist effects dampen sound.

A car door thumps;
leather soles clip asphalt.
I might myself be mounting toward
that lofty white bedroom
where a girl once strode about
in hairclip and shirt, and nothing else.

3

She liked it sudden;
she liked it from behind.
And to touch herself, impaled,
and get her fingers wet –
to watch it being done and done to her.

Mirrors, jellies, spunk:
she dug the lot.

4

We were often hungry.
She'd grind her teeth
as she dealt with her black orgasms.
While the bare wooden floor shone with cold
and night filled all the windows
with ink immaculate,
rain might start to fall
on sill and foetal punga,
on plants like wrecked umbrellas
in the garden where a man had lost his life.

## ASTRONOMY

As the Requiem begins,
I feel an old unease.
*"Blood of my Saviour,*
*Bathe me in Thy tide . . ."*
My cousin describes his father's life.
In Japan after the war,
Clem had been appalled by the destruction
and seldom spoke of it.
A dozen old soldiers lay poppies on the coffin;
the Last Post is played
while the priest swings his censer.

Slipping away from the after-match function,
I board a train for home.
Beyond the window, night,
the black star-maps of suburbs.
If I were asked, I'd say:
"We're a couple of billion freezing
light-years removed from God."
Gothic or baroque, our steepled yearning
to be more than we are
is trivial, amoebic.

## A LYRIC

Autumn is dusk, brings dusk,
dusk's grave adjustment of tones.

I have bathed, my fingers smell of money.

Greyness, stillness, chill —
each is rich in itself.

The sea has fingers like these smallnesses,
these notes; those who are cold
it touches with odours.

Behind you hung a vast fund of cloud.

There dwindles on my eye
your eye, the charm of clavicles.

You were as real as meat, as thunder.

## POLYGON WOOD

*(Polygon Wood gave its name to the*
*second of the three Battles of Ypres.*
*My grandfather survived it.)*

"From tents on a plain
we were tempted out. To embark for this,
not yet all mud.

"Mother, I am lost,
am lost inside a map you enter through
a hole in a hedge."

Soon winter will come and snow seem to repair
this medieval convent.

Because he is clad he is ready.

Because he is clad he deflects.

He will move forward untouched
through all that is neutered and still.

## OPPORTUNITY

I think of rooms,
high-ceilinged and airy,
in which live single men.

It is morning.

Here chairs have arms
of coarse green breadth
and icons are pictures
cut from magazines.

It may be that water
winds into a basin
with a noise suggestive
of rinsings, dabblings.

Escape would make
as small a sound.

# THE MARITIME COOK

Here lupin hides lost items
of the ocean's rusting tackle.
Beyond these chains and flukes
is a bach I have my eye on,
a shed built into clay
and roosted in drab flax.

Feeney was once in a film
with Ustinov and Mitchum.
When he came into The Grand
it was with a toey shuffle
he made seem heroic.
Black Irish, square-templed,
he had a broken nose
the shape of a pawn or key.

He burned himself to death
with magnificent negligence.
Among the many things I seek,
the many reliefs I crave,
is illusion of the imminence of rain,
the first scant scratches of drizzle
on asphalt or pane.

## SNAKES

It will take three hundred years
to clear Cambodia of unexploded mines.
Most of my friends have gone –
to London or Sydney.

In Australia's tawny wastes
people build houses, carefully assemble
settings of rock and water,
plant saplings with blue leaves.
And lo the water runs or falls
or otherwise imitates the artificial,
Zabriskie Point, its stilts
and black mirrors. Snakes lately infernal,
slim yellow tubes much dyed and printed upon,
admire the baffling water.

A man like a grocer, damp-jowled
and horn-rimmed, dangerous captor and killer
(the man who loved a corpse
because of its passive ways),
speaks of his crimes with deference and tact.

Freud defined mental health
as the ability to love and work.

There is chaos on the roads.

It is winter in Khandallah;
it is winter in Kilbirnie.

Rain leaps in a spray
from streetlamp to streetlamp;
wind gusts with a hoot through wires.

She doesn't want me, no,
but what do I do with her ghost,
that yellow hint of herself
she has failed to take with her?

There are wormholes in time.

There is darkness over an ocean.

## iNSOMNiA

My doctor has explained
that for years Churchill couldn't
or wouldn't sleep at all
except in startling bursts
of a few seconds duration.

In order to take them
just as directed,
I must first physically count
all hundred and ninety-six pills.

Then the fridge packs up
with a shuddery anal wheeze,
kwee-chit-shit.

Once I was stung on the lip
by a radioactive bee,
once when shifting a wardrobe
I swallowed a wasp,
and once a strange girl
tried to bite my tongue off
when I kissed her.

I think of Tycho de Brahe,
fastidious Danish astronomer,
who wore a golden mask
and fumed through it.

## MY ELDERLY FATHER WATCHES TELEVISION

How can he sit there enjoying the cricket
when there's death to think about?

## PILE DIARY

### Day One

There's disorder down there.
Tenacious muscles
pleat and pucker and pop.
Axiomatic too
that if I want to adjust
there's an Arab in the car park.
I go for Doctor Unguent
and ride home in a cab
with forty dollars' worth of Xylocaine.
The sky's a dish of creamy lime delight
forecasting needles, blades . . .

### Day Three

"What can you tell me
about X?" she asks.

It's Sunday. I'm in pain.
I have to sit in a certain position.
"He was once in the navy," I say.

"He uses *little* words," she says.
"He asked me to suck him off.
I'd like him to fuck me
without a condom."

In the absence of God and soul
and any afterlife,
sex itself becomes holy.

## Day Five

Tomorrow, the op.
I'm frozen in the act
of giving birth to grapes;
as the hours pass,
they tarnish and dry.

The clues of the crossword
make a surreal poem.
I'm a cast baboon
presenting her bulging vulva.

## ILLNESS AND RELIEF

A curry roll and chips for tea.
It's morning now, and cold.

In 1986, the German Expressionists
came to the waterfront.
I bought the poster depicting
a jackal-headed creature
reared like a man on goatish legs,
jagged, shaggy-ballocked.

The steroid's pianism taps my flesh.

\*


I concluded long ago
that life was terrific, wonderful, sublime.
Having won a couple of million bucks,
who could feel otherwise?

\*


I bathe in numinous joy.
I'm washed in it – truly.

And I've always known about
that contrary black will in the body,
that organ hidden in among the others
which sleeps or closes down . . .
and then begins to tick again, as now.

My innards twang and sluice.
I creak like a sailing-ship.

**LORE**

From the dew's many inventions
falter white lights like pins.

In sleep we recover
things perfected by loss.

When I was a kid
I invented a word for fire.

I didn't know that when a flame is snuffed
it merely goes elsewhere.

## THE FIFTIES

Those were afternoons
as grey as stones.

There were mushrooms in the hills
beyond the Riding School.

Our father came from the tram
beery and rich with shillings

but these were afternoons
as numinous as graves,

the fishing-boats unmoving
on water slow and bleak.

## EUCHARISTS

Eternal light
would shine on us,
the blessèd.
To breakfast
on Christ's body
was to eat redemption.

Later in the day,
boys growing up
from the waist down
lifted themselves
from the school baths.
Beneath the skin
of their wet thighs,
muscle pushed at muscle
as if with appetite.

The anal pong
of sodden togs.
Navels dribbling
spidery plumes of hair
(all I ever wanted
was to mix my metaphors).
Todd swung his meaty dork at me, alas.

Perpetual light
would shine on us – or not.
The sorriest wore glasses
with one lens plastered over.

# KILOHERTZ

The horsey air tosses.
The nostrilled air and peppery outdoors
prompt a rush of freshness to his brain.

These are magnolia;
they dangle ruptured, shaggy-stamened things.

A carnal ticking fleshes, lengthens him
but he's finding Roy Street soothing.
At number twenty-three there lives a chap
who produces radio programmes in his bedroom.

## CONSOLATION PRIZE

I bring them home
on the bus, a
cluster of small
pink roses.

I shorten their
stalks with scissors
and put them in
a pickle jar.

They swell and fade;
each time I look
their petals seem
more numerous.

# RADS

## Beyond the Pale

Her face is broad,
familiar as light.
She's altogether
blonde-maned and modern.

Defied, I dream
an African surrender
(envenomed arrows,
spears and penis-sheaths),
the anxious gut-to-gut
of darkest betrothal.

## Rads

Smooth crimson bomb of lipstick

Skin-coloured glamour, powdery

Faint odour of stocking,
of leather, of foot

Yes, lots of brief exposures

Like too many X-rays

Till I begin to cook

## Blonde Mischief

"You surround yourself
with sexual propaganda."

"Nonsense," she insists.

I believe her. Sort of.

She peeps out at me
from behind her golden hair.
"Anyway," she says, "I never fancied you."
It's *this* I can't believe.

*Now we embrace*

*We seem to be embracing*

*But she turns her head away*

*She holds her mouth away from mine*

## Ben-Hur Signs His Autobiography

When by chance I see her
at the right hand of Charlton Heston,
she's a snowy altar,
she's an acolyte in white
whose smile sends me to hell.

**He Seeks an End to Passion**

No room for *me*
on her busy sexual schedule!

A pinch of clockwork drops out of my tooth.

*

She belongs to all the others.

(I write in order to have
degrees of clarity –
if not solutions, legible diagrams.)

She belongs to all the others. I consent.

## THIS MORNING'S VIEWPOINT

Slow fans revolve,
big clovers of blade.

My purpose was to kiss her.
You'd think a man of my age
might have pulled *that* off.

My hearing improves
when I put my glasses on.

When this whole show is over –
when the cosmos has used itself up
and is dowsed like a match
in a saucer of cold coffee . . .

The birds are going deaf.

Misery is contemptible.

## WHISPERS
*In memory of Henry O'Neill Cochrane, 1923–98*

*George Gershwin died on July eleventh, but I don't have to believe it if I don't want to.* John O'Hara in 1937

1

Police halt the bus
and send us on a detour.

Late in spring,
hours of glittery rain.

Water has collected
in the luggage rack;

measures of water spill
when the vehicle corners.

Through all the commuting involved
in this long goodbye,
I've worn the one pair of pants.

2

The nurses have left him
with a bare bottom.

There is the penis
with which he fathered me.

His useless legs have taken on
a yellow, waxen look.

This is what you get.
Yes, this is what you get
for simply having lived.

3

The question I frame,
the question I *put*, is this:
"What's it like in there?"

He mouths a word, two words.
My father seems to be
in a place of great safety.

I test the word "safety",
its applicability
in this strange context.

4

He can sometimes manage jokes.

Full of air and quiet,
the words he so painstakingly constructs
lack all plosive force.

The speech therapist
has forbidden him liquids.

There's a redness on his cheek,
a self-inflicted welt.

Of what he was, there's only a fraction left,
the sketchiest of sketches.

5

A card arrives from the blokes
of the RNZAF Association,
*Per Ardua ad Astra.*

In two shades of blue
with specks of red and gold,
their monogram suggests
a cloudless alpine sky,
an uncrushable turquoise gem.

6

I tune the black transistor
to the rugby.

Less pained today, my father drifts off,
his mouth becoming an old man's O,
a black round by Munch.

And all at once the sun
whitens the room, turns its vernal flaring
on my suspect dad.

Perhaps he dreams of running.

7

Left alone in the house
I play *The Best of Bing*
tracks my father liked

"It's Easy to Remember" (Rodgers and Hart)
"Sweet Leilani" (Owens)
"The One Rose" (Lyon and McIntire)

> *Don't leave me alone*
> *I love only you*
> *You're the one rose*
> *That's left in my heart*

8

Stephen and I
drive to the lake.

There's a bunker with slits
signposted *Men* and *Women*.
Waving its many legs,
a huge, varnished beetle
lies on its back in the urinal.

Ducks and geese surround
the parked cars.
We drink from squeaky polystyrene cups.
It emerges that my brother
believes in heaven.

9

*And Niam calling Away, come away:*
*Empty your heart of its mortal dream.*


It's somewhere between one and two a.m.
My brother the nurse is holding Dad's wrist,
taking his pulse continuously.

"He's arrested," says Phillip –
and the big shift begins.
But our father shifts from life to death
without so much as a sigh.

And this event is hugely ordinary,
both more and less dismaying
than I'd expected.

10


The sleep-out clanks and wheezes.
In even the slightest wind,
a plum tree's laden boughs
graunch roof and guttering.

The day after my father's death,
I fetch a ladder, scramble up into
a noiseless green twilight.

I saw, sever, grapple,
drag a big fork to the ground.
And with it falls a crop of firm green plums
soon to brown and split,
soon to begin to feed the starlings.

93

11

During the night, it pours,
it really buckets down

My dead father listens

My dead father listens but can't hear

My dead father scowls like an infant

12

Now for the final act, the private cremation.
We dash to the porch through sizzling rain.

I happen to know that the undertaker
is a piper in a pipe band.
This very afternoon, I'll see the priest
eating an ice-cream in a cinema complex.

A newish Union Jack
has been draped across the coffin,
a mess of paper poppies heaped on top.

The Whispering Glades muzak
with its tune by George Michael
seems to fit the "Nazi" style
of the building itself.

I knock on my father's gleaming lid.
And I think of his abandoned wardrobe,
the suits and shirts on hangers,
the garments he'll never again fill.

## MILESTONES

1

Between the city and me
was only an ancient door
I'd painted orange.

Mounting treacherous steps,
Peter Olds brought sausages and plonk.
The wardrobe contained
a thousand and one empties.
In the fullness of time,
someone would smash the big mirror.

2

My father dies;
I'm diagnosed as having . . . never mind;
my longing for a leggy journalist
is slowly starved to death.

Yes, where I heal I'm bland.
A coffee bar provides
festivity enough, my daily fix.
I read the blackboard chalked in limes and pinks:
*Obey your thirst –*
*Bacon and Eggs, $6.00 –*
*Extract me the soldier from the sputnik.*

My melting moment tastes of garlic.

## EFFECTS

My dying father, dying,
cast off all disguise,
fled the scene
of his last impersonation.
An old man for a month
(cross, deluded, firm),
he'd no taste for the part.
He left behind some ties,
some socks and shoes and things.
And I wanted to send them on;
I wanted for an instant
to forward him his stuff.

## WORKSHEET #2

Bought new clock.
Put broken one in rubbish
where it ticked.

\*

Writer Terry Southern's last words:
"What's the delay?"

\*

Lying in the gutter, a peacock feather.
Once, the ace of spades.

\*

It takes me nearly fifty years
to come to love my life.
And then I dream I'm nursing
my father's childish skeleton.

The skull's but a rotten little shell
all sticky and caved-in.
And then it's loose and can't be put back on.

\*

The Botanical Gardens.

On a bough above the track I'm descending,
a bird I'd thought extinct,
last seen in tiny profile on the sixpence.

It wears a cravat.
Its bass note has an eerie timbre:
fencing-wire guitared.

## ZIGZAGS

And what was the city to us
if not a sweet protracted sacrament?
As innocent as grunts we headed out
determined to know the foul & fair of it,

its driven rain & rosy overcast
its murky brass & panes of clouded ice
its lights imprisoned by steel grilles
its altars knobby with bluebells & snails

its Roxies/Ferris wheels/recumbent lions
its small octagonal tiles of black & white
its Chinese restaurants with tanks of carp
its pantographs & blue cascades of sparks
its swimming pools of blood & fiery cloud

And oh to drink those mists & foggy glares,
to feed one's living face to that dark conflagration
streaming ever blackly in upon itself,
to that smooth rapid vortex of combustion
streaming ever blackly in upon itself,
and oh to merge one's own pluvial heart
with greenish dawn & aqueous rainbow

As swart & lean as soldiers we took on
vodka/acid/Mandrax/tequila/smack
drowned in shallow puddles of neon & oil
conferred with fallen anaesthetists
overdosed suavely in purple bedrooms
jumped in flapping coats from viaducts
discharged our wonky liquorice shotguns

saluted the golden breast of the Lizard King
froze to death in sanctifying snows of white noise

(An X-ray of a flea-pit in the badlands
revealed the fuzzy souls of methylated cops

Because I was a poet people died
Because I was a poet, people died

## PERSIMMONS?

Drawn by the green windfall,
she sneaks inside our fence from time to time,
a lovely Vietnamese hungering for something.

And she stands on the path
in the shade of the queer-looking tree
to taste of the fruit she can't resist.

Her infant asleep in its chrysalis of thongs,
she kneads and sucks the pulp
from somewhat spiky gourds,
a slender and oblivious invader
feasting blamelessly.

And the thing is *this*, you see:
I don't know what she's eating
and have no use for it.

## SEVEN PIECES I'D LIKE TO HAVE WRITTEN

1

You go to the door. You halt, indecisive.
The blaze without is not for you just yet.
*Summer's gaudy din intimidates.*

2

The hallucinated cat skips and skids,
cuffs and slashes like an hussar.
*Woe betide the mouse, the chitinous cicada.*

3

With an oily clack of hidden nether switches,
the bus comes to a halt.
*And what of the moment when death seems remote?*

4

The dog in the canyon shivers,
barfs its meal of moonlight and flowers.
*The air is wet where it was hewn.*

5

Couples do tennis. Tourists disembark
to photograph the roses.
*A grief is an echo of a grief.*

6

His toothache a sour electric spurt,
he buys himself a brandy.
*His enterprising son has pinched his dope.*

7

*Crème de menthe* and candles.
Her telephonitis warms a beige handset.
*Across the ceiling, bearded kings parade.*

## ACETYLENE

*Fog in the street*
*and at the intersection.*

On a moon called Triton,
snowy volcanism,

stupendous jets
of liquid nitrogen.

*Fog in the street*
*and at the intersection.*

The welder's gas combusts
in pinpoint laserblaze.

His black coat saturate,
a solo Lab' in polka-dot bandanna

waits for the lights to change.

Roman numerals
& spiky carburettors
clog the drains.

As I pass the Cenotaph,
a cold wind soaps my cheek.

Red leaves bounce like crisps.
The shawled & hooded dead
thirst no more nor hunger.

# ANZAC DAY

*Time slips by; our sorrows do not turn into poems;*
*And what is invisible stays that way.* Mark Strand

\# The southern sky is chilled by stripes of cream and teal.

\# The term **dada**, the French word for "hobby-horse", was selected from a dictionary by Tristan Tzara, Hugo Ball, Jean Arp and others. In Zurich. In 1916.

\# I'm simply a maker of things. If I didn't make poems and stories, I'd paint pictures. If I didn't paint pictures, I'd fashion wooden toys, coating them in bright enamels.

\# **hobby-horse** n. 1 a child's toy consisting of a stick with a horse's head. 2 a preoccupation; a favourite topic of conversation. 3 a model of a horse, especially of wicker, used in morris dancing etc. 4 a rocking horse. 5 a horse on a merry-go-round.

\# "Man may, indeed, have evolved from the primordial ooze, and that may be accepted as good if we assume that it is good to have complex life on earth, but this again is an arbitrary assumption."

\# The southern sky is chilled by stripes of cream and teal. All the old soldiers are bones, diminished tallnesses slung in hammocks of soil.

## UNDER THE VOLCANO

Not a drop of alcohol
in eleven years,
but still I dream
the same old shame,
the same old prideful shame:

I'm living in a single, basic room
with just a one-bar heater,
a mantel radio, a knitted tie of peach,
a stolen copy of Robert Lowell's *Imitations*
and a flagon of lunatic soup . . .

and one day I'll be taken out and shot.

## THE BASICS

Every day, I walk
from Berhampore to Molesworth Street,
buy my few supplies,
come home on the bus.

If not exactly a hunter,
I'm a *gatherer* who covers many miles,
smiles at babies
in supermarket aisles.

## VANILLA WINE

Above discoloured seas,
the potters and the painters are at work
in furbished gun-emplacements.

\*

My uvula's been mangled,
my gums adroitly darned
with bristly twine:

the periodontists call it
*a full clearance.*

\*

Could this be a new beginning,
an end to thoughts
of waning and stagnation,

of gulls, decrepit junks
and orange suns?

\*

HAPPY CHIMPS ARE PROBLEM-SOLVERS!

My flat becomes a speech laboratory:
"\*?$!%!&_ . . . "

\*

The shunted clouds pile up
in livid scoops,
podgy helpings garishly backlit.

I cleave to the delights
of custard and marshmallow
and dunked biscuit.

# THE MAN IN THE AVIATOR SHADES

i

Night. Rain frisks the window.
His Glock's as hard and fat
as a Coca-Cola bottle.

ii

He drives to the airport to buy
a box of Durex Fetherlites,
a yellow baseball cap.

The Mazda's awash
with table knives, screwdrivers,
Rosicrucian pamphlets, flying manuals.

iii

His foods are soups
and chocolatey desserts
straight from the can or punnet.

He works with blades and glues,
crude little stumpy little brushes,
kiddies' printing kits.

The papers he creates
by the light of a Hanimex lamp
are handsome and fishy.

111

# BUNKER BULLETINS

1

The Chinese pagoda
of an antique chimney-pot,
its flame-blue glaze reflecting
a sky remote and grey.

2

Odours of stone
and cold water. Of bad drains
and Cold Water Surf.

This is the prayer I'd pray if I believed:
*Qualified failure is sweetness enough.*
*Confirm me in it.*

3

In The Coffee Bean,
smoking's permitted
and I light up.

"I've quit," says Gerry, "but
a bit of *pass*ive's good."

4

The car steers awkwardly.
At Rongotai, a grounded DC-3,
its cockpit higher than its tail,
its skin a tinny mirror.

"I put a DC-3 in my novel."

"Of course you did," says Lindsay.

5

To movies.

*Jesus' Son* with Billy somebody.

In films about the Seventies,
they seldom get it right.

In those golden days, any man possessed
of even a scintilla of narcissism
grew his hair as long and wavy and lustrous
as he could manage.

*

Next to Video Tonite, a pharmacy.

The good apothecary
sells me a brace of Microlax sachets.

6

Sufficient unto the day
are the two-minute noodles thereof.

7

The nerdy little bloke
across the road
has quit his corner flat,
taking his cat with him.

The cat would sit
in the window, in the sun,
licking its gloved fists
or watching what it watched
through mustard eyes.

A *black* cat, rather thin.

But *there* . . . every morning.

## THE POET

The plants are tropical;
a cleft rock spills municipal water.
Just outside the gates of the embassy,
security guards with mirrors fixed to poles
examine a Mercedes' underbelly.

His life's a convalescence –
a slow, elated, awed recovery
from humiliation.

The embassy intrigues him.
Noon has dumped itself
in the rich, exclusive compound,
a precinct shrill with the white noise of cicadas.
Surrounded by hydrangeas, a matt-white satellite dish
audits the lives on distant planets.

Not far from where he sits, turquoise locomotives,
urns in alcoves high in brick façades.
Transparent and intractably remote,
his childhood has somehow been installed
in the air above the city.

*Awed recovery from.*
And this glorious day in summer becomes
something he can use.

# ERIK

## 1

Pince-nez. Bowler hat. Pointy wee beard. He always carries a black umbrella too. Man Ray says he looks like an undertaker.

## 2

A dingy closet two metres deep, Erik's room is a rubbish tip. The pedals of his broken-down piano are tied up with string. "Sometimes he plays at night," his concierge reports, "but he doesn't do it loudly. No one complains, since it's only Monsieur Erik."

## 3

His erudition is claimed to be patchy and eccentric. Some say he's like a man who knows only thirteen letters of the alphabet and decides to create a literature using only those letters.

Well, Erik does away with bars and time signatures. He "decongests" music. He concerns himself with showing beauty absent – in a world without love, beauty absent.

## 4

It's rumoured that Erik remains a virgin. Nor will he get a job.

## 5

His gaze is one of satanic acuity. He tells Chalupt his librettist, "Be short and precise. Present novelty. Speak with authority, without arguing."

During a rehearsal of Socrate, he says to Calvocoressi, "It's all very simple. You can see what I'm trying to do here – originality through platitude."

## 6

He's fond of the writings of Hans Christian Andersen. Flaubert's *Salammbô* inspires the *Gymnopédies*. And Erik discovers Péladan, author of crank religious tracts and founder of the Ordre de la Rose-Croix Catholique, du Temple et du Graal. Of this quaint brotherhood, Erik becomes the official composer.

## 7

He makes notes with a propelling pencil. Italian terms like *dolce* and *mezzo-forte* he replaces with his own suave inventions: "while watching oneself approach"; "with a fear of the obscure"; "astonishing and convenient".

## 8

He likes apples and alcohol. His friends are Brancusi, Derain and Milhaud. Brancusi cooks for his guests in his sculptor's kiln.

## 9

Erik's liver is diseased. Erik's liver is diseased.

(Cirrhosis is common among natives of Calvados. In Erik's case, this predisposition has been aggravated by the difficult circumstances of his life. Often reduced to dependence on hand-outs, he has not eaten frequently nor well. "It's odd," he muses. "You find people in every bar willing to offer you a drink. No one ever dreams of presenting you with a sandwich.")

## 10

*"I don't regret anything. I've never written a note which didn't mean something."*

## 11

As he's lying very ill in the hospital, Brancusi brings him yoghurt and chicken broth. The nuns feed Erik champagne – oh, and paregoric elixir, a camphorated tincture of opium.

## 12

He dreams of the yellow clouds of Honfleur and Le Havre. He dreams of himself in the sailor suit of his boyhood. He's attending a regatta, is fascinated by the many flags. He knows that some of the smaller ones spell out pithy nautical cautions. Their colours float in bits on the choppy blue water.

## 13

The evening of July 1st, 1925. Having received the last rites of the Church, Erik dies.

## 14

Conrad S., Robert Caby and Darius Milhaud go to Erik's room.

Hats and walking sticks. Piles of old newspapers. A parcel delivered many years before but never opened. "Nothing worth a shilling, says Milhaud.

Behind the piano, Darius discovers an exercise book containing *Jack-in-the-Box* and *Geneviève de Brabant*, which Erik used to claim he'd lost on a bus.

## 15

His funeral is attended by his neighbours. Someone has arranged for a wreath of salmon-pink roses and hydrangeas. The sun shines.

## 16

COCTEAU: One day I met Erik crossing the street in heavy rain. His umbrella was under his arm.

MILHAUD: Quite. When the sly old coot passed on, three members of his family came to visit me. The weather was perfect, but they *all* had umbrellas!

## (17

Erik's grave in the Arcueil cemetery was to be marked by his great friend, Brancusi . . . but never was.)

Savvy meters clack their blank eyes shut.

No one arrives and no one departs;
the walls are full of dice and knucklebones;
mice snack on quiet's little bongos.

When aqueous day eventuates
and light lies like water on the tiles,
yellow birds will sip
from morning's shallow stoup.

## THE PICNIC

In the ancient Russian film
made in an age of clockwork and leatherette,
my grandfather's wearing his Sunday best
and sitting on a beach.

He's holding his mug out for more.
More *what* remains a mystery.
In silent conversation with herself,
my grandmother ignores him.

Though the film is Chekhovian and swart
(the end of the world is but
a frame or two away),
this Perce looks somewhat sharper
than the man I came to know –
like some rare crake significantly doomed.

## LOOP

Foals were born beneath
the great chart of the stars;

I woke to the sepia smell
of wallpaper parched and friable;

gilled, waxen, large,
Kurt's mauve erection
swung like a derrick.

For many years,
I steeped myself in booze.
I steeped myself in booze
till even my marrow drank,
but it's all behind me now,
sad fuck that I am.

## HAY STREET

We weren't in love
we never pretended to be
but I did my best to feed you
I did my best to feed you

Remember the ants in the sugar bowl?
And on the wall a tree of antsy ants,
a xylem and a phloem yes of ants?

Though the hall outside our room
was dense with oaken fruits,
varnished nuts and berries,
we were often hungry:

once we dined on an unsuspecting guest,
his plume of belly hair
slim as a smoke signal.

We weren't in love
we never pretended to be
but I did my best to feed you
I did my best to feed you

## THE PLUNGE

How much of me was bone when last we met?
I'd quit a dour, monastic safety;
I'd come down from the mountain of myself

to an unfamiliar street, above the which
an angel's airy form decayed and stretched.
How much of me was bone when last we met?

To where a ghost of sky and vapour mixed
was hoovered ever slimmer by the sun,
I'd come down from the mountain of myself,

had made the loser's masochistic plunge
into bewitchment, funk, gaunt hankering.
How much of me was bone when last we met?

Though loud infatuation's crass alarm
still buzzed and blurred my very skeleton,
I'd come down from the mountain of myself

to your repudiation. (Yes: it was *you*
I'd fallen for, you salt-and-sugar minx.)
How much of me was bone when last we met?
I'd come down from the mountain of myself.

## DREADS

That briny pong in Bond Street.

Saint Mary of the Angels' sapient façade.

Those blue X-rays the trolley buses botch.

*


It's a glossy, *Playboy* winter
of bloody neon and big coats,
odours of soap and chocolate.

I buy a couple of pencils,
3B Staedtlers made in Australia.

My father knew his pencils.

*


They'd left me alone with his body.

He looked newly youthful.
He looked newly healthy and relaxed

but would very soon be off,
would soon be setting out . . .

and I wanted childishly
just to go with Daddy.

I was forty-seven.

\*

I'm seated in a coffee bar at last.
A scrawny but attractive kid comes in.

*Wispy beard, two-tone dreads,*
*face of a savage tabby baptist.*
Looks as if he's strayed
from a stripy production of *Cats*.

Have a nice life, kid.

## IMPERSONATING BONO

*for my sister, Mary*

On a bright, crisp day in winter,
we leave our mother's house to walk to town.
You seem proud of me. Or unashamed. Which is better.
You hook your arm through mine and we are sweethearts.

Petite and fresh, you're over from Australia.
Left to my own devices,
I'd walk as far as the old railway station,
passing the junk shops and the new green tractors,
the saddlery with the plastic horse on its awning.
But not today, for today I have *you* on my arm.

Our jaunty tour takes in
the carpeted mall, the TAB Dad ran,
the library in which you once worked.
In Paper Plus, we score a couple of Little Golden Books
to give to Luke at his christening brunch
(the reason for our unseasonal reunion).

I've left my shades in Wellington.
You talk me into buying
a replacement pair at the $2 Shop –
slittishly repulsive retro jobs
through which the cheapened world looks sick and blue.

With your light hand on my sleeve,
I feel a sort of massive buoyancy.
"Time to be getting back?" "I guess it is."
So we breast that special zone of trainless hush
above the ginger-gravelled railway line.

And here it is before us, colourless:
the dour, adult, dismaying mystery
of why we must live apart, as if divorced.

## EVOLUTION

The pipsqueak chime of lightcreep.
And myself somehow dawning,
patiently coming about.

*

The honeyeater family consists

*

Fly me to the Kimbell Art Museum
in Fort Worth, Texas.
I want to stand before
secular altars;
I want to touch the naked aliens
shown on television
(they smell of expensive lubricants.
Their slender plastic shoulders
are gorgeous).

*

The honeyeater family consists
of 173 species.
Remember too that birds
are the brittle wee derivatives
of the dinosaurs.

## THE PLAIN SPEAKER

She lives in a house of cats and bric-à-brac
and ancient little books in pinkish threes,
clothily faded Hazlitts or Brownings.

"Shall we take our tea outside?"

Sunlight on a glass-topped coffee table.
A pear tree feigning mattest, blackest death.
"He's not as big as K_____," she says,
"but I seem to be thriving on the change of semen."

"I'd forgotten how quiet the country could be," I offer.

She risks a sort of stiffish purple smirk.
"K_____ was almost *too* big, of course.
Did you ever see the shameless sod engorged?"

## HYPNIC JERKS

Treble piggy graunchings:
a freight train bumping through
the centre of Levin.

*

Hair Say

Electric Ink

Phoenix Garden Restaurant

And being here once more
means reacquaintance with
this shallow silver platter of an ashtray,
a small vintage Studebaker
mounted on its rim.

*

A movement in the bushes.

Cat or bird?

It's a hedgehog, a long one,
blondly whiskery and purposeful of stride –
a *sen*ior-looking cove.

*

131

Greeny Celtic gurgles from the roof.

The rain's a sweet, narcotic sort of gloom
congenial as wine and candlelight.

Beset by somnolence and hypnic jerks,
I could be happy here.

## FEAR OF FLYING

And it dawns on me that I'm fond
of putting things behind me.

*This* looms, and *That* is coming up . . .
and I wish these events were over.

There's even a sense in which
I'm in a hurry to be through with living –

a sense in which I'd like my very life
to be over and done with. Sorted.

## BLACK PAN

*A poem commissioned by the Museum of Wellington City and Sea*

We were urban hippies then, the best of us,
Landsmen with embroidered bell-bottoms.
But you couldn't live in Wellington and not
Know seamen and the murky sea itself,
The sloppy, spitting greenness of the harbour.

Its odour was fruitiest in winter.
You'd only to turn down Waring Taylor
On your way to the back bar of the Midland
In order to encounter it anew:
An oystery pong of dredging and beached kelp,
Of ancient drains and briny nether sumps.

Peter drank rum and five-ounce beers.
His boxer's nose was dentedly baroque.
The goatee and the slim dark suit
Combined to lend him a brooding, Spanish air.

He mentioned once *The Sundowners*
And being in a scene with Robert Mitchum,
But he seldom spoke of his maritime career
(Which a nasty quayside accident had scotched),
Except to explain what a black-pan menu was.
"No more significant bells for me," he said,
"Unless we count the last damned bell of all,
The one that tolls as I'm going up in smoke
Like a snarler left in the deep black pan too long."

# LITTLE BITS OF HARRY

## chapter i

The Marmitey smell of a roast.
Harry watched his Grandad crank the table.
*June could do with a spot* and *Here's to your very good health.*

## chapter ii

He was raised not far
from a salt-and-vinegar beach.
The wound in his shoulder looked like a slitty eye.

## chapter iii

Harry had a friend called Brian.
Brian's smile was framed by inverted commas ("v").
Together the boys made poisons,
decanting their grassy sauces
into Aspro bottles shaped like canteens.

Under the house was where
they'd built their Zombie Chair.
And under the house was where they stored their poisons,
smoked cigarettes and cultivated stiffies,
tent-poled their school shorts with stiffies ("v").

## chapter iv

Trust Harry to do a lovely Jesus.
To get himself nailed up
with many a fine contortion and grimace.

(The theme from *Exodus* played.
Brian's Roman helmet had been painted
with gold paint from the hardware.)

### chapter v

Harry's father loathed Mario Lanza.
The cold yellow sky dimmed to mustard.
Rain swept up the valley, crowding it like troops.

### chapter vi

Winter seemed to mirror
the sweet rainy gloom
in Harry himself.

Nanna sat in front of the fire,
toasting her shins and listening to the footy.
Harry sprawled beneath her, in the odours of crumbling heels,
mottled calves and droopy puce stockings.

And the wound in his shoulder began to squeak,
squeak and whistle like the fire itself.
Like the fire in which the damned were said to live,
their hot bodies molten orange jellies.

### chapter vii

"That's it," said Harry, vexed. "I'm setting my face
against it all."

"What about your passion-plays and poisons?"
his mother asked.

"I'm setting my face against it all. All except swimming and going to the pictures."

"Well that sounds mighty fine, but what about the dental clinic? You won't get very far setting your face against the dental clinic, however implacably."

And when he got to the brilliant, methylated clinic,
he was sent straight home again
for having furry teeth.

"I've disgraced us both," Harry told his mother.

"And how," said she. "Get in there and polish good,
you fiend!"

## chapter viii

The wound was like an eye.
Or a slitty, sticky mouth.
Whether eye or mouth or merely perennial gash . . .

## chapter ix

Harry's father managed
a radio shack in Furnace Lane.
And Harry liked the murk,
the smelly alchemy of his old man's profession.

There were fresh boxed valves in pigeon-holes
and chassis labelled like toes in a mortuary.
And Harry was thrilled by the tinny stink,
the runny splash and flash,
the quicksilver dartings of the solder.

By the bevelled tongue of the iron, so hotly blued
and silvered.

"The secret of good soldering
is to work cleanly with clean surfaces,"
Harry's father explained.
And handed his son a slimmish book: *Radio for Boys*.

### chapter x

College. Saint Cuthbert's was a place of "standards".
Of lines to be toed and traces
not to be kicked over.
Larking near the milk float merited a flogging.
There was also a mysterious urinal
juniors were discouraged from using.

When Harry ventured into it,
he got what almost amounted to a fright.
The gorgeous prefect Harry encountered within
had long-lashed, Ray Liotta eyes
and a dingy, ancient, ox-felling cock.
A veritable Trojan of a tool, but modelled in accordance
with the slickest principles of modern rocketry.

### chapter xi

Each year began with the soapy odour of newly purchased
exercise books. The chaste white leaves of which seemed to
offer scope, to promise better academic results. It was never
long, however, before Harry had begun to fill his books with
circuit diagrams and sketches of inventions. With red stanzas
shaped like expensive bits of advertising copy.

### chapter xii

Brass band. Choir. Drama club.

Harry tried them all, only to find himself
underemployed and bored.

And then would come the warm messy business
of withdrawal, disengagement.
The qualified disgrace of having to return
the flugelhorn whose valves had kept sticking.

### chapter xiii

Firemen pumped Saint Cuthbert's flooded basement.
In library and classroom, flubby gas burned pinkly.

And the body of a pupil killed in a car crash
was laid out in the chapel.
And the guy looked most peculiar,
bounced sideways into death,
like some rouged harlot lividly contused.
Like some rash pierrot mauled
by the colours rose and mauve.

### chapter xiv

A morning, yes, in spring.

But Saint Cuthbert's lay in ruins,
Saint Cuthbert's had been crunched.

A haze of smoke and dust
hung above a hill

of shattered grey masonry.
Puny yellow fires devoid of any briskness
licked up through the rubble here and there.

I loved it but it didn't love me back, thought Harry.
It failed to apprehend the qualities in me,
the excellence of me and my lambent wound.

### chapter xv

Or were the failures and derelictions mine?
But were they?

### chapter xvi

Parks and public gardens became his haunts,
a limp oilskin parka his cloak.

In a stately filmed ascension screening backwards,
he was sinking to the bottom.

### chapter xvii

He'd noticed a dank garage
up near the old tram tunnel.

Seepage and stink and frog-green slimes:
no one had used the place in years.

And Harry took his fish and chips in there,
his library books and cartons of flavoured milk.

And the hip, punchy novels of P. Zanoski
got into his blood like a craze,

a suave new malaria
sexy as ejaculate.

### chapter xviii

The odour of a sump or an oily grave. But Harry rehabilitated a manky chair he'd found (so that then he had a seat). And he stole a couple of P. Zanoski's books and fashioned a shelf for them (so that then he had a bookcase). And Harry liked to imagine P. Zanoski flying in from Chicago. Sending one of his minders ahead of him. "P. Zanoski will be here in two minutes. He'll accept a cigarette, but please don't offer him gum." The white gleaming limo just outside, soon to be joined by a second and a third.

### chapter xix

The telly he salvaged from the skip? The telly he salvaged from the skip was a small girly number with a plastic cabinet of cream and lipstick-red. It needed a few modifications, sure, but Harry worked for hours to convert it into a sun-lamp, and soon he had his contraption up and running. And he'd spin the bicycle wheel that juiced the system, strip to the waist and sit in front of the screen. Certain dormant circuits would thaw and kindle, and the charcoal screen would glow invisibly, pumping forth a torrent of black light, black influence, black medicine. And the wound in Harry's shoulder could begin to heal at last. Could begin to shrink and close – or seem to.

### chapter xx

Unworried sleeplessness.
Engagement with the texture of the moment.

For the treatments had their novel side-effects.

A good dose of the sun-lamp
imbued him with an energetic bliss,
a wakeful equilibrium,
a rapturous serenity abiding.

Yes.
A single hit of darkest radiance
and Harry was pumped for days.
Wired and feeling like
a crystal ping sustained.

### chapter xxi

Night's brassy shadows.
The flimsy Chinese carpentry of night.

And Harry out walking all the time,
working off his treatments at all hours.

### chapter xxii

They stopped him outside the electricity park, that buzzing necropolis of cottage-sized transformers and giant porcelain peppermints.

The car drifted in toward the kerb like a flying saucer on its best behaviour. "What. You couldn't sleep?"

"Something like that," said Harry.

A golden-haired forearm. The dashboard's toxic purple array. "Hop in," said the cop, "it's fun in here."

"Like *Der*. Like *Let me think*."

"You're a healthy looking kid. And a smart one too I'm told."

"So?"

"So give your folks a ring. They're worried sick. I speak to you again I better hear you called."

### chapter xxiii

Weeks passed. Months.
While slowly the sun-lamp's dark effulgence
seemed to dwindle in potency,
so that Harry needed more and more of it.

And then, while he was out,
the garage was trashed.
The bicycle wheel wrenched from its cradle.
The telly's ham-shaped tube bashed in
and its fragrant pastel gasses dissipated.

### chapter xxiv

Slipping his P. Zanoski books
into his khaki bag,
he traipsed across the city.
Cowled and caped in blankets,
he hunkered down beneath the motorway.

A spitty wind blew up.
The sky was a fuzzy orange murk.
And it rained on our dispirited Harry,
on Harry and his army-surplus knapsack.

## chapter xxv

He took to drinking cough mixture. Sometimes he was asked to sign for it. "Blaise Cendrars", he'd put. "Blaise Cendrars" or "Alexander Trocchi". And he'd get through several bottles in a day. Three or four bottles, yes.

## chapter xxvi

He'd often breakfast at the soup kitchen (a statue of the Holy Family presided. The soup came in stainless-steel jugs) and there he met a chick who took him aboard a ship.

In a grotty cabin charged with a greeny stench (some sturdy distillate of marine putrescence?), he gave her the business well and truly. "Great," she said, "and you so long and thick! Do you always keep your shirt on?"

"It's gelid as, down here."

"*Give* us a swig of your syrup, there's a pet."

## chapter xxvii

3 a.m. A brilliantly fluorescent service station. Harry had scored a cappuccino (he craved the milk, the sugar) and was stirring it with a small wooden stick.

"So how the fuck's it looking?" asked the stranger.

Harry shrugged. "Like where do I go to sell my blood?"

"You don't do that. You make another plan."

"Yeah?"

"Sure." The stranger winked and popped his can of Pepsi. "Stick with me and I'll get you hung."

"The word you want is hanged. Stick with me and I'll get you hanged."

"Hanged. Hunged. Whatever."

### chapter xxviii

His name was Rubin.

A little tee-shaped chalice of a tuft
adorned his lower lip,
and he wore a long black leather coat
in which he looked agreeably satanic.

### chapter xxix

He was staying at the swanky Xanadu. "Temporary riches," he explained, "– a winning streak at blackjack."

Carpet. Tepid musks. An elevator prescient and swift, below the perspex capsule of which the twinkling city was spread. And Harry saw the city and the world (a doomed winter festival of lights) fall away from under the rocket.

### chapter xxx

Rubin's suite was warm, its colours peach and beige. Rubin himself had hired the ecclesiastical jukebox with its rainbow of glows.

Harry took off his parka. Unbuttoned the cuffs of his shirt and sat down on the sofa. "I could get used to this," he said.

"You reckon?"

### chapter xxxi

When Harry produced his bottle of cough mixture, Rubin scoffed. "Say goodbye to that crap. Let me give you a taste of something decent."

He tied off Harry's arm with a rubber tourniquet. And slid the needle into Harry's vein adroitly, painlessly.

"You're being very . . . *doctorly.*"

"I keep it dark, but I *al*most qualified."

"And I won't need the linctus anymore?"

"You won't need the linctus. Nor any fucking sun-lamp."

"How come you know about the sun-lamp?"

"I had a hunch. I've read my P. Zanoski."

### chapter xxxii

The drug in Harry's system was a liquid clarity. Was prompting him to level, spill the beans.

"I have a wound."

"We all have wounds."

"But mine's peculiar. Peculiarly mine. It weeps and shines and sometimes even murmurs."

"Don't they all."

### chapter xxxiii

A liquid, improving clarity.

And Rubin was transformed, in Harry's sight. Transformed and transfigured. Laundered and sharpened.

The Ray Liotta eyes became apparent; the smile framed by inverted commas emerged ("v").

And Rubin unbuttoned Harry's shirt, gently baring Harry's dubious shoulder. And his lips sought Harry's wound, in order to kiss it better, in order to seal and heal it with a kiss.

**FOG**

Four nights of lucent hush, the airport closed

I slip into my poacher's coat
and brave the toothless flux

## LIQUORICE STICKS

I spot it in the Salvation Army thrift shop:
Young and Willmott's *Family and Kinship in East London*,
a Pelican which seems to have been lightly toasted.

In the old British movies, people smoked
during meals. And the films and novels of that time
had melancholy titles, names evocative
of bricks and soot and drizzle,
the pensive clarinet of Acker Bilk –

*Billy Liar*

    *A Kind of Loving*

        *This Sporting Life*

            *Saturday Night and Sunday Morning*

           *There is a Happy Land*

## WORKSHEET #6

The television says, "When covering up a murder,
use clever plans."

*

Blemishes accumulate.
Hair gets ever thinner.

I'm beginning to look like
Homer Simpson's father.

*

In his tiny cape of loudest ginger checks,
the vaudeville moth is sleeping it off on the pelmet.

*

Anything can happen in life, including nothing.

*

Being both sly and meretricious,
the act of writing seems to me to resemble
the colourful felony
of counterfeiting banknotes.

# IN MEMORY OF MARY THERESE KILKELLY

Make it short and sweet, I told myself;
Though only the plainest words
Will carry to where she's gone,
Tell of the clip of Marie's
Twinkle-toesy trot.

Keep it short and sweet, I told myself;
Though only the plainest words
Will carry to where she's gone,
Tell how Marie's eyes were of
A stratospheric blue.

Every death is a Calvary.
The men go first, the husbands and the fathers –
"How fast has brother followed brother,
From sunshine to the sunless land!"

Every death is a Calvary.
Our thin ranks get thinner by the year.
How fast has sister followed sister,
From sunshine to the sunless land.

# NEGATIVE BUOYANCY

## Choice

Consider the "philosophy of freedom".
Which consists in being aware
that a choice made now, today,
projects itself backwards
and changes our past actions.

## Between Drinks

He rides the coach toward
his father's alcohol.
He twitches and bleeds
like a mangled insect.

The bus is an imperilled submarine
maintaining radio silence.
Perhaps one wee green light
nipples the dashboard.

Pouring past outside,
a long black nowhere nothing.
Pouring past outside,
ton upon inky, analgesic ton

of time bought, of reckoning postponed.

# Taking Stock

In the early days of my sobriety, I made an intriguing discovery: if I simply *pretended* I'd downed a double gin, I could almost feel its sedative effects.

*

Abstinent for more than fifteen years, I've forgotten the magic of alcohol, forgotten its heat and radiance, forgotten why I followed its smoke-blackened banner for two long decades, my fealty unalloyed. Forgotten too my own capacity for exuberance. Forgotten how engrossing, *HOW ABSORBINGLY INTERESTING IT IS TO BE DRUNK!*

*

I was once a guest of the Salvation Army. They ran a camp for inebriates in the Akatarawa Valley.

A courtly old piss-artist and Faulkner lookalike, Joe used a tortoiseshell cigarette-holder. "I'd buy a case of whisky and send my wife to her sister's. An understanding woman, my dear Cath."

Logging trucks and misty stands of pine. Jehovah in the amber beams of noon.

Tania chewed her nails, admitting to nothing. "I miss my children. I don't know what I'm doing here and I miss my children."

# Negative Buoyancy

His brain had been irradiated, seared.

The morning after. And the room in which he found himself was as cold as a quay, a bus stop. He lay on a couch in an unfamiliar room and tried to keep his mind at a semi-submerged level. Tried to maintain a negative buoyancy.

Odours of sebum and dust. The couch's fabric had a bummy, sebaceous smell. His brain had been exposed to some bleaching flash, some obliterating power surge, but the tepid consciousness of a doomed mountaineer was all he'd need today.

He heard a scritchy sleet paw a window. Grey grey grey. Cold cold cold. His dimly remembered "hostess" was staying in bed, thank God. But he'd failed to hide a bottle and all the pubs were shut.

Sunday. The obdurate fact of it. A grey smeary fate he feared and hated. Each hour of which was itself a little Sunday – or even a Good Friday. For dolorous and bleak would surely be the stages by which his need for a drink would grow, becoming ever more shrill and urgent, ever more direly biochemical.

His brain had been washed by some obliterating flash. He knew himself to have been cancelled, deleted, rendered white. A Sunday in the very trough, the deepest pit of winter, and he knew himself to be incapable of his usual hustle.

There'd be no fix today. No medicine. He was all out of schemes and all out of fight. He was all out of fight and all out of options.

## PANIC IN THE PARK

I quit the path and dodge across the grass;
I duck beneath a bough and graze my scalp,
but a tall, flaccid panda corners me.

"Hi!" he offers brightly.

"What do I have to do?" I ask.
*"But what do I have to do to avoid you?"*

# DAYDREAM

I'm parked on the main street
of some strange, distant, Agfacolor town

in an Agfacolor dusk (maroon, particulate)
with rain beginning to fall,

with tiny dirks and chevrons
of rain on my windscreen.

A massive freight train skips
its massive iron skip,

passing behind the paint shop
and the lawnmower place,

and I'm lost and found and lost
and on the sauce again;

I'm lost and found and lost
and on the turps again,

and oh the large narcotic
sweetness of my crime!

## COCHRANE ST

The dark side of The Warehouse.
An outpost of the RNZAF
and Fulton Hogan trucks behind wire mesh.

*In Cochrane St, in Cochrane St,*
*the gulls and sparrows play,*
*but surfers and dog-walkers tend*
*to go the other way.*

# CHEMOTHERAPY

A marquee stocked with gleaming cheerios.
Children and a friendly, broad-backed dog
(table to the kids' unmannerly elbows).

The tall man with the little paunch is ill,
but we're here on this blustery coast
to celebrate his fifty-fifth birthday.

The wind-minced sea has darkened.
It's time for the cake with the single candle,
but the northerly has strengthened
and the candle can't be lit;
taking the cake from his daughter's hands,
Nigel pretends to blow
the unlit candle out.

His wobbly gait is not yet a totter.

He's touched and grateful, but also very tired.

The wind-minced sea has darkened to purple.

## STARSHIP

Gareth and Chris and Peter are dead,
but some of us remain.

Lindsay is planning a life
he can fit into a suitcase:
he'll sell his books and buy
a wafer-thin laptop. "With a Compaq,
you can sit in a McDonald's
and beam yourself about.
Wireless communication, boy!"

And the ship we're all aboard,
the starship in which we're passengers?
A vast constellation of globes and tubes,
she resembles a molecule,
the massive model of a complex molecule.
Her architects cared nothing for her looks
and her profile is anti-aerodynamic,
but she glides through time and space
(through wispy time and unresisting space)
with huge serenity.

## JUNGLE ALTARS

Abundant rain in billows,
sifting down like smoky wrathless wrath
on St Mary of the Angels.

\*


Every good book has a gun in it.

I think I'll go with the 7.65mm M48,
a Hungarian copy of the Walther PP pistol.

It differs from the original
only in the placement
of the loaded-chamber indicator.

\*


The deep seriousness
of the priests who taught me –

who has it now?
Where has it gone?
Does Donald Rumsfeld have it?

## MOTEL

The blue lights of the Airport Motor Lodge:
they cobalt me; they penetrate and stain;
they send me, yes, and bring me back again.

## PENINSULA

The grasses hereabouts
are the grasses of Long Island,
the wheat-coloured grasses of a junkyard.

\*


I prefer the short to the long,
the minor to the major. *Bartleby* to *Moby-Dick*,
*A Portrait of the Artist* to *Ulysses*.
I even prefer the fascinating programme booklet
to the film festival itself.

\*


The jumbly dining-room
of the Loong Fong suggests
a steamship's not-quite-kosher saloon,
the brines and greenish fogs of old Shanghai.

# BASHŌ IN THE BATH

### i

There's a certain chilly moistness in the air.
A whiff of ginger too,
of sugared ginger and wood shavings,
as if an exotic crate
were being unpacked nearby.

### ii

To lie in a steaming bath
and look up at a pane
in which there glows a sky of Easter-blue

is to feel the great wheel turning,
is to feel the great wheel turning.

### iii

He's no longer young but not yet old.
When he looks in the mirror
he sees scarring and staining,
the sagging of accumulated fats.
What he sees in the mirror
has been too long in the sun,
too long in the wind –
too long in the smokehouse of life.
There's ruin in that face
(gravity being both strong and patient),
but also a sort of overelaboration,
a poofterish embellishment
of indifferent features.

What to do with such a face?

He shaves it here and there,
barbers it a bit.
While scowling at its asymmetries,
its blue notes, its descents into bathos.

iv

Bashō in a ditch
with tyres and shopping trolleys
longs for mist and rain,
the aqueous smear of a distant village.
Its strong green chlorophyll.
Its fawn smokes and glistening slates.
A place he's never known
but was at home in.

v

Rotting fronds and broken red canaries.
Mangled trikes and fish-shaped skeletons.

One soldiers on, of course,
having seen the movie.
*Despite* having seen the movie.

## THAT WINTER WITH CELESTE

I don't remember buying this espresso.
I don't remember last night's television.
I don't remember Troy
nor the first dynamo
nor the first use of ether in dentistry.
I don't remember coal
nor the skittish Tiger Moth
nor Romeo's cute little hard-on.
As well as all of which
I'm struggling to recall
that winter with Celeste
in her bed above the harbour,
the ships like chandeliers
parked beneath her window.

# LUNAR CAUSTIC

i

Bashō on the road
and headed north.

*They've shot me full of sings*
our subtle bard has sung.

ii

Bashō passing through
the steel towns and the tin,

the brown smokes and the black,
the neon steams and gentle acid rains.

And he finds he likes the crummy local bars,
their argon *STEAKS* and *COCKTAILS*,

their baizes red and blue.
And he feels himself replete

with a sweetish sort of lostness,
a sweetish sort of anonymity.

# ENQUIRY

At the end of what long road
does Bashō get to play
with Rod Stewart's train set?

## SUPER WINE

The news is early or his clock is slow,
so he grabs his mug of tea and pops
a biscuit in his pocket,
the top pocket of his faded old coat.
It's a wreck of a thing, this coat of his,
a shamefully limp and grubby article,
but he wears it through the news and *Campbell Live*
and on into the night,
and he wears it when he leaves his little flat
and slips up the lane and out onto the park
and lights a cigarette
(his skinny nine-o'clocker
and the last of the day).
And he smells the smells of mown grass and woodsmoke,
and he walks across the park toward the lights,
the lights of the houses on the hill,
secular stars of silver and orange,
and he walks beneath the frosty stars themselves,
this unmarried, unmended man,
this unmarried, not-unhappy Earthling,
a Super Wine forgotten in his pocket.

## EGYPTIAN SILHOUETTE

1976. My first book of verse
was a handsome, stiffish thing,
its detachable blue jacket
loud with Egyptian Silhouette.
As good as a bought one, yes.
And I took it to Levin on the Newman's.
As how could I not.

\*


A pearly summer sun.
My sister's Fleetwood Mac on the stereogram.
Dad had read my book, and he offered me a beer.
"You'll never make a poet," he said,
"but you might have made a bloody good painter once."

"I haven't touched a brush in years.
Anyway, I could never draw like you."

"No."

"I couldn't."

"No. But you had a way with paint,
an ability to hint at distances and depths."

"Did I?"

"Hell yes."

## WINTER

A tepid rain's puce music.

Mice in the bread and mice in the bed.

See one police car and you'll soon see another.

# LATE IN THE DAY

## i

Myself on the radio.
I sound like a slithery old wizard.
You can smell the plastic teeth and lung disease.

## ii

My writing life has been
a series of defeats.

Soft defeats.
Invisible defeats.

# ANALGESIA

i

The Haz Mat yard sleeps yellowly
and the airport talks to itself,

addresses itself
through a tinny megaphone.

ii

It's pleasant here at dusk,
even when the sucky silver shrilling

of tall cowled jet engines
carries on a gentle southerly

to my back door,
the porch on which I'm smoking

a friendly cigarette,
a soothing cigarette not yet my last.

iii

A new *New Yorker*,
inkily sweet-smelling.

Tonight's heroes are
Denis Johnson and J. M. W. Turner.

iv

I'd like my work to be
all the things it's not,

but each of us is stuck
with his own particular schtick.

(Beyond a certain point, effort makes no difference,
effort simply deforms.)

v

The irritability
of the adult animal:

I saw it in the steely eyes
of poor blue James Galvin, visiting poet.

vi

I amount to something, yes,
as I almost failed to do,

and there's satisfaction in that.
But one gets older and outlasts ambition,

tires of the game of living and being liked,
outgrows the need for people.

And one becomes the vessel
of an odourless boredom,

and sex or one's imagining of sex
somehow detumesces. Becomes dilute, diffuse.

The fleshly gloss goes off it;
its potency's dispelled

and its magic drained away;
the sinful sin of it is driven out,

leaving just the colourless molecules of indifference,
the watery hormones of analgesia.

## ANDROPAUSE

A moon aswim in the glow
of an odourless odour – its own.

*

All my dreams recall
the thrills and serenities of booze.

*

There are no glittering prizes.
One sobers up and knuckles down and so forth,
but there are no glittering prizes.

# THREE SONGS

## 1972

Clear Light, Purple Haze,
talk of Aldous Huxley.

Buddha Sticks, Black Bombers,
news of William Burroughs.

## The Duke of Edinburgh

We drank our gins and jugs
at the slovenly old Duke,
its malty carpets moist
with a sticky sort of filth.

The walls were mustard
and the carpets charcoal,
but knives were seldom pulled
and not much blood was spilt.

Come closing time, we ate
(if we were lucky)
at the greasy Golden Spoon
just up the road –

sausages and chips
or sweet-and-sour pork
(white bread with salt and Worcestershire sauce
were meal enough for the poorest).

The cook had an eye
like an oystery egg
bungled in the poaching,
but his dishes were good.

**Holy Water**

The rain was ancient then,
sweeping and abundant,
and the churches we'd forsworn
somehow kept us straight,
even as the rain blackened them,
slicked their slates and filled
their high, greenish gutters,
brimmed their verdigrised and gargoyled troughs.

# THE ROOMING-HOUSE

1

An ambulance might splash
its scarlet light about.

The concrete steps and paths
were mounded and Pompeian,
like fluid porridge frozen;
*Do Not Leave Chotes To Soke* read the card
in the cold, spacious, primitive laundry.

2

When I *got* a room at last, it was tiny.
Tiny and quiet, with a wee built-in bookcase
in which I installed
a radio and a dictionary.

And I sat side-on
to my little olive desk
and drank and drank my plonk
a little at a time,
like a student of something large and long,
large and long and complacently abstruse.

And many nights fell
and many days dawned,
and I studied and studied.

3

An ambulance might splash
its scarlet stain about.

My bedding was arranged
neatly on the floor,
but my sherry glass got very
cloudy, grubby, gooey, its utility contingent
on its never being washed.

Yes. And what I was after,
what I sought to renew day after day
and night after night
(tried to understand by reinforcing),
was the gorgeous condition of being
addicted to addiction.

## THE LICH-GATE

My life was mine as coins are brown and few,
As the weak and enchanted fail to thrive,
And the undertaker's fattened roses blew.

My housemates were junkies and transvestites;
Sweet Cilla could flash a daunting tool;
My life was mine as coins are brown and few.

The oblong clock had stopped at 3:15
(Whether a.m. or p.m., there was no knowing),
But the undertaker's fattened roses blew.

In his own diurnal dark, some Druid prayed for me
(This was the dim sense I had of it):
My life was mine as coins are brown and few.

There on the corner, funeral home and clock.
Beyond, the city's arsenals, coffers.
And the undertaker's fattened roses blew.

So, as Neil Young sang his hurricane of need
In the lit and brittle bottle shop replete,
My life was mine as coins are brown and few
And the undertaker's fattened roses blew.

## ROBIN

He was taking a break from busking.
Taking a break from having to stagger home
with guitar and amp and buckets full of cash.
And he wanted to write a book,
he wanted to write his autobiography.

First things first, I said.
Begin, I said, as you mean to continue.

So we went to the typewriter hospital
and bought him a reconditioned Brother (forty bucks).
And I gave him a great quantity of yellow foolscap
and he set himself up at the kitchen table.

Typing at all hours.
He'd be typing when I went to bed
and typing when I came down to breakfast.
How do you spell psychosis? he might ask.
And what about chlorpromazine?

Keep typing, I'd say. Nothing like typing
for improving one's spelling.

# SAFFRON AND SALT

I wash my plate and light a cigarette
and sit through the galling news
from home and abroad.

A three-year-old girl is tortured to death
for being ugly.

There's no correcting anything. Short of wholesale
slaughter.

Better to walk away, walk out across Crawford Green
just as the sun is setting.

\*

Guadalcanal. Tulagi. Halavo Bay.
My father was a radar mechanic.

They didn't salute on the runway.
They didn't wear their sparks, in case they were captured.

*Sparks.* They didn't salute or wear their sparks.

\*

I pass the pharmacy, the Four Square,
the Acropolis Fish Supply.

On a warm, pre-Christmas evening,
the smell of curry rolls being deep-fried.

My father worked and raised his kids and died.
And there's no reclaiming him,
no getting him back from the air.
No gathering his smoke,
no shaping his smoky semblance.

# CHINESE WHISPERS

The white speck of a gull
against a thunderhead.

\*

She took me to the airport
to tell me what she was doing.

Bleak and dark the runway, the wastes.
A sky of puce with sooty anuses.

Airports are for getting abortions.
You fly out in a storm
And return empty. You fly out through a storm
and return immaculate.

\*

My brother came south in a storm.
To a dearth of light, a paucity of warmth.

He's finer than me, my brother.
Newer, browner, better.
Monk's mahogany skull, Zhivago specs.
At the bottom of his pack,
tobacco, yellow Zig-Zags, mobile phone,
but also his "well-thumbed" Baha'i missal.
And he sat on the floor and opened himself
to the splendour and the scent,
the fragrant wind of belief and belonging.

# AGES AND AGES

# I've lived through the age of terrific movies.

# I've lived through the age of Tiger Balm
and books about Paul Klee,
and I've lived through the age of rain
on dustbin lid and onion flower.

# I've lived through the age of the crumbed sausage,
and I've lived through the age of the typewriter
(that simple machine you could fix
with a table knife and a small green can
of machine oil, oval in cross-section).

# I've lived through the age of rat and rot
and wearing rags to court
and wearing rags to funerals.

# I've lived through the age of flea and louse,
of friction-burn and crusty meatus,
and I've lived through the age of fawn wallpaper
and sepia suicide.

# LINES IN PURPLE INK

*for Fergus Dick*

The Stabilo 0.4
is a yellow pen with a purple cap.

*

Thunderheads. Stormlight.
Our elderly neighbour's out on the lawn.
Our elderly neighbour's out on the lawn,
and he's sweeping it with a kitchen broom
like a Berber sweeping sand
from a highway in a desert.

*

The splayed umbrella drying in the bath.
The swish and sizzle of the airport's wet tarmac.

*

Our windows leak and weep.
Our whistling seals are sodden.
We paint by numbers, build model aeroplanes.
Our mothers stare at our shoes, but we have no shoes.
Our mothers stare at our shoes, but we have no mothers.

So much of life is duty.

The best you can do is trim your beard
and show up on time.

Show up on time, count the house,
have a word with the technician
about the light on the lectern.

## PINKSHEET #2

Forward. Through the minefield.
But I tinker less, make fewer "improvements".
Have become more respectful
of my first draft.

*


The battered vintage spaceship
hovering in bad light above the city
is not unlike a rusty old reservoir,
a grimy old gasometer.

*


*Certaine Small Poems Lately Printed*

*


That murdered Spanish poet too
involves himself in this,
gets into what I'm doing
here on the page, pencil to paper:
I glimpse his black fedora
and glossy jaguar.

## TIE AND TYPEWRITER

I think I liked it better
when I hadn't yet been unearthed,
when I hadn't yet been shone on.

\*


I was living in a room
at the old police barracks,
and I'd pinned to the bulletin-board above my desk
a blackly shaggy chimera by Richter.

My mornings were a blissful convalescence,
my nights a rapturous buzz
of tea and cigarettes and prednisone.

Nor had I pawned my dove-grey portable.

\*


Here I am in a tie.

A skinny, yellow, cub-reporter's tie
worn at half-mast.

And my "full set" (my beard)
has photographed very black.

\*

I think I liked it better
when my mornings were a blissful convalescence,
my nights a rapturous buzz
of tea and cigarettes and prednisone;

when I watched from my third-floor window
the fireworks and the firemen on the hill,
the tinted smokes of a ghostly battlefield.

*

In winter, it gets later earlier.

And that particular winter
was long and dark and wet,
was somehow rich in comforts, fascinations:

men in orange slickers laying pipes,
odours of leather and doughnuts and brine,
mercury vapours and aluminium steams,
beads of rain englobing carmine sparks.

A winter and a city
rendered in the oiliest of chalks.

And a steroid kept me awake for days on end.

And mine were avid, science-fiction eyes.

# BASHŌ BEGINS

### i

Bashō digs the city
and the city digs Bashō.

He hangs with Sting and Moonbiscuit Smith
down by the waterfront
(low dives, you understand, are where it's at).

### ii

Big warm bears patrol
the CBD at night.

Shortly after dawn,
the rippling, rinsing wash
of hope renewed.

### iii

Bashō cleans his teeth and combs his hair.

Tea and Hemineurin for breakfast.

On a wonky old typewriter,
he writes *The Book of Sin.*
On a wonky old typewriter,
he rides through rain toward a ruby smash.

# DREAM SONGS

### 1

There's nothing to be done
and nothing to be had.

There's nothing to be had
and nothing to be done,

but I dream a dream in which
I'm on the turps again

and a rancid angel woos me,
coveting my bottle.

### 2

A chilly wind had dried the streets.
They kept the sherry in the china hutch.

Inebriation's bliss. Inebriation's blizzard.
Every night of my life, I dream that I'm carousing,
dream that I'm faceless again.

# THE LAST OF BASHŌ

### i

Bashō writes of the purple wine he likes.
Of the barman's slim syringe and black nail-polish.
Of the ten-dollar note burning in the ashtray.
Of the silver airship moored above the pines,
the tethered airship going nowhere slowly.

### ii

The snide sirens dive and the rain catches fire,
but what of the Bengal engine's mango afterglow?

### iii

Bashō alone and walking some high path.
Bashō alone and climbing the concrete steps to heaven,
a flask of gin in his satchel.
A flask of gin and a spring roll gone cold.

## PINKSHEET #7
*for Denis O'Connor*

Haloed lamps in a misty, sodden park.

\*

Canticle and psalm and holy smoke.

\*

The white noise in the cabin
dissolves, absolves, dissolves . . .

The black light in the cockpit
absolves, dissolves, absolves . . .

\*

"One should always travel in a business suit."

## SUMMER

*If it might be said fairly that you have*
*hopes and fears, would you say you*
*have more hopes than fears, or more*
*fears than hopes?* Padgett Powell

For summer seems always more or less sudden.
For the wild geranium is coral-pink.
For my little bit of a garden hasn't flourished.
For monarch butterflies enliven the morning.
For they do this silently, but silently.
For the birds out there look angular and fell.
For I'll be sixty next birthday.
For I haven't stopped smoking yet.
For the tigers of wrath are wiser than the horses of instruction.
For Gerry has moved into his new pad.
For Moonbiscuit Smith is singing sweet and low.
For Moonbiscuit plays the ancient billabong.
For Gerry's yellow *tuk-tuk* is dotted with tiny decals.
For people no longer read Jorge Luis Borges.
For summer's rusty gravels are enduring.
For summer's orange lichens are abiding.

# MIXED FEELINGS

i

Sixty today. I'm sixty today.
And though I've been sober for more than twenty years,
I still have nightmares about
failing to make provision,
failing to provide myself with booze.

ii

Sixty today. I'm sixty today.
A triumph of something over something.
A triumph of modern medicine over natural defects,
organic flaws and pregnabilities.
(I should have died in my thirties.
I *did* die in my thirties – and more than once.)

# PIBROCH

*The chromosomal abnormality*
*involved in Down's syndrome*
*is trisomy-21, or the presence of three copies*
*of the 21st chromosome.*

Funk and Wagnalls New Encyclopedia

i

My little brother is dying, and I . . .

I wish that it were me;
I feel no great reluctance to die, myself.

ii

My little brother is dying and I,
not consciously believing in God or prayer,
say a sort of prayer for him:
*Oh let it be easy and total,*
*easy and total.*

iii

David Joseph Cochrane.
The chrism fresh on his forehead.

My little brother is dead
and lies on his back on his bed at the home,
a little old man very grey and pale,
very cold- and bloodless-looking.

iv

My little brother dies
and I spend the night in a room
thick with the floral pong
of some noxious exudation
so putridly vile it stifles me.

## WONKY OPTICS

I'm under the influence.
I'm under the influence of influenza.

Yesterday, I sat in this chair and did nothing,
sat in this chair in the sun, dozing and dreaming,
dreaming and dozing,
my hot blood squishing through my plastic head
in effervescent pulses.

Today, the same, except that I try to reread
Joan Didion's blue book
and have to keep stopping because
I can't see for tears.

Cheap tears. Easy tears.
Tears big and round and grossly magnifying.

# TELEPHONITIS

## 1

Tu Fu flips open his cell and speed-dials Li Po's number. "I've been spinning my wheels," Tu Fu confides.

"So drink," Li Po suggests. "So drink and fornicate and do narcotics."

"Spinning my wheels and running on empty, of late."

"So get yourself a kick-arse tattoo."

"Is this the toxic dusk at the end of Literature? Are our centuries of effort at an end?"

## 2

Tu Fu flips open his cell and speed-dials Sinbad Greene. "I've written nothing for weeks," Tu Fu insists.

"Perhaps you're trying too hard."

"Possibly. Probably."

"Make use of what presents itself. Or chill and learn to wait."

"Make use of what presents itself?"

"Yes. And remember – First Thought Best Thought Always."

"You can't possibly believe that."

"Believing it makes it true."

## 3

Contemptuous of time zones and expense, Tu Fu rings Wang Wei.

"I"m working on a screenplay," Wang reports. "Here at The Pink Motel, it's always noon, and today's a photocopy of yesterday."

"Let me ask you a question, friend. How many books do you love?"

"I couldn't say. I'd have to have a think."

"Just how many books do you love, old son? But really and truly *love*, finally?"

## 4

Tu Fu flips open his cell and decides to go for broke. "Paint me a picture, Maestro, if you will – a picture to inspirit and inspire."

"Glad to oblige a colleague," says Mark Strand. "I'm sitting at a table at the end of a white pier. An orange sun is sinking through the carnage in the west; it tints and taints the sea"s busy surface; it tinctures the decoction in my glass and slightly stains the front of my white shirt."

"And what are you quaffing, Mark?"

"Ambrosia. With ice. The dead in their grey pyjamas know the last ship has sailed, and I'm drinking the nectar of the gods."

## THE GREAT WALL CAFÉ

The major gave us a chit
and we took it down the road
to a basic Chinese joint in Ghuznee St.

1974? Our not entirely wholesome covenant
would end when I got drunk,
bought two bottles of Glenvale's sweetest sherry
and caught the train to Auckland.
Meanwhile, we had a room and not much else.
Meanwhile, we had one another.

Eggs and chips and white bread in abundance.
Worcestershire sauce in a faceted, pressed-glass shaker.
And we paid with our Salvation Army voucher.

Her breasts were small but boldly, starkly nippled.
She was avid and game, my golden-skinned nymphet,
and she had great faith in me. She had great faith in me,
and together we'd admire my splendid erection.
Her breasts were small but loudly, brownly nippled,
and I fucked her frequently, but frequently.

# OUR CITY AND ITS HILLS
*for Bill*

The steampunk city's Buddhist rain
Is marvellously hushed
It always thus affects my brain
And stops me getting lushed

The steampunk city's Buddhist rain
Wets rooftop flue and tank
It makes me want to catch a train
And ride through cuttings dank

The steampunk city's Buddhist rain
Is not unkind to cats
It falls on cenotaph and crane
And blackens many hats

*Some put their faith in sleeping-pills*
*Or brash domestic wines,*
*But the rain has altars in the hills*
*And cloisters in the pines,*
*The rain has altars in the hills*
*And cloisters in the pines*

# THE VIEW FROM ATLANTIS

oh luscious oils & inks,
night's blackest inks & oils

*

munted sputniks burn,
the dirty-penny buzz
of blood salts my tongue,
and things will get worse
before they get worse, no doubt

*

white winter's silent shout has stilled the town,
but the ancient bough puts forth
brittle-looking flowers,
small blue blooms like arid asterisks

*

our bodies are made of water

our bodies are made of brine and fleet wee sparks,
tiny electricities that flit,
twitchy barbs and darts that beep and ping

# EQUINOCTIAL

A hand's turn or two.
A hand's turn or two
and my work is done for the day.

*

Behold my suit of meats
and fat tarantulas. Check out my cloak of knives
and pinkest heliums.

*

Our lilies are broken by the wind.
Broken by the wind, and then they rust.
Broken by the wind, and then they rot.

*

A habit I seem to have formed (and can't afford):
each morning at eleven, a latte at the same place,
at the same table, my own inviolable spot
downwind of the non-smokers.

Coffee. What a racket. I must be nuts.
But I'm making an attempt to *live*, you see;
I'm conducting an experiment in living.

## STOPPING

The clot on the lung
and the dot on the clock. The dot on the clock
at which he stopped.

\*

A cascade of failures, and then . . .

When I woke this morning at six,
Gerry had been dead for more
than twenty-four hours.

(*23/12/12*)

## CONSECRATED VESSELS

The idea of eternity
intrigued me. Forever
and forever, and then

another forever.

*

The *skirl* of a tram departing.
The stately *wade* and *underway* of it.

(Put me in a chamber and bathe me in
the odours of fish and chips and tomato sauce,
of salt and salty sand and Coppertone,
and you'd recreate for me
the Island Bay of my boyhood.)

*

The hill burned on which
Hitler hid with his sticks
and dribs and drabs of wire.

His sticks for signalling,
his few slack rusting feet
of barbed wire. Burned

like a circus. Every summer.

*

207

The Holy Ghost was everywhere.
The Holy Ghost was everywhere,
but everywhere invisible, unfelt.

*

(I'd seen a film in which a circus burned.)

*

Chalice and ciborium
were consecrated vessels,
and eager altar boys

must never touch them.

# GOD AND OTHER WORRIES

But how to get through a life
without making things?

*

Nevil Shute. Hammond Innes. Alistair MacLean.
Were popular authors back in the 1960s.

*

Bertrand Russell's refutation of Aquinus?

If it's logical to posit the existence
of a cause without a cause (God),
it's just as logical to posit the existence
of a universe without a cause.

*

Cremation happens too soon after the event.

How can we be sure
that death has taken place,
even when death has taken place?

*

The starving mother pleading for milk,
but begging for milk for her dead infant –
she's there in Herman Melville's Liverpool
and she's there when the British enter Belsen.

*

and as the heat in the furnace builds and builds,
a point is reached at which the coffin explodes
and the burning corpse sits upright suddenly
with its molten head ablaze

*


But how to get through a life
*without making things?*

Time and materials, yes:
these are what we need
and these are what we're given;
we choose our silver rods and golden wheels,
and then we build our spidery gizmos.

# SERVICE

I'm sixty-two, it seems; my mother's still alive and *compos mentis,* and it's dawned on me that I'm probably not going to die *soon,* that I've probably got a few more years to serve. A few more years to serve in Pharaoh's army.

Not that I've forgotten being younger. There I was as an ambitious young novelist, as hot a self-believer as ever was, but I wasn't able to build a readership. And that slow-motion failure was like a slow, protracted mugging.

I never quite *took* as a novelist, no. And what I do in the recuperative quiet of my failure is write poems. Poems, little fictions, mini essays. (I don't enjoy worrying. But worry, nontheless. And my lightish workload matches . . . my shamefully unadult lack of stamina.)

## PUBLIC RELATIONS

My barista asks me where he can find my books, and I'm not exactly thrilled by this development. My barista thinks I'm a great bloke, currently, and I don't want him reading my books and changing his mind.

## OVERHEARD

Scots College blazer, prefect's badge.
A slenderly sturdy six-footer, dark.
He's walking briskly with his head held high,
his cellphone pressed to his ear,
and this what I can't but hear him saying:
"Don't do it. Please don't do it. Please don't do it, please."

## WHAT THE POETS TOLD US

Chips and eggs in Chinese restaurants.
But we read, we had our poets.
The earth was blue, like an orange;
a Māori Jesus walked on water;
kings in golden suits rode elephants over mountains.

# ORIENTAL SKETCHES
*for Carl Shuker*

### I

*Even I love this season*
*of new kimonos.* Ontsura

The tūī cluck and chortle.
Cluck and chortle lots.

### II

*Bones on the moor.* Bashō

With bones on a moor,
The poet need not mention the moon:
The moon is roundly, pinkishly implicit.

### III

*A chlorinated twilight by Magritte.* Li Po

The magpies living in the Norfolk pine
Don't envy me my mug of tea,
My two or three malt biscuits.

# IV

*Plastic daffodil and wooden Buddha*
*are the things of morning; at night I go in search*
*of neon gate and hydrogen jukebox.* Tu Fu

I've been fighting with my ancient, arid pillow,
A thing as hard and flat as a mummified cat,
And the side of my face is bruised.

# V

*Two petals fall*
*and the shape of the peony*
*goes all to hell.* Shikibu

The novelist and his daughter,
His little daughter warm and portable –
She fiddles with his chest hair
And calls him Carl, safe in the arms
Of a good, friendly, durable father.

## THE PLAN

My Testament will feature Sennheiser headphones.
Chocolate fish. Baboons and saveloys. *Vanity Fair.* A yellow
bathysphere. *Degenerate Art.* Old Spice. Ernest Hemingway.
A blasé cat (unkempt). A wee blue light of great sincerity.
Daffodils and carburettors. Diamonds and rust. Khandallah.
Savoury mince on toast. A red ukulele.

My brother will come to town and I'll put him up
at the Intercontinental.
We'll have a week of films and galleries,
partake of lemon slices served
with oodles of whipped cream.
And Stephen too I'll tip
into my slender book,
my lithely unambitious Testament.

# YOUNG NICK

The city's betwixt and between. Warm and quiet, empty and becalmed. Suspended between one year and the next. The city today is Herman Melville's Manhattan, Herman Melville's Wall Street on a Sunday.

My barista's called Nick. The last time we spoke, he was off to see the new *Star Wars* film. "How was your movie?" I ask.

"Awesome. Outstanding."

"You were worried about J.J. Abrams' involvement."

"I was worried about J.J. Abrams' involvement, but he's done a terrific job."

"Good. I'm glad."

"And how's life treating you?"

Life? I can stand it. Continue to be able to endure it. "Goethe said that the idea of suicide had gotten him through many a bad night."

Nick's smile is undismayed. In terms of personality and style, he's bulked up winningly in the past few months. A savvy, cheerful kid with a good heart, he's growing daily in confidence and sophistication.

## ON REACHING A CERTAIN AGE

How far I've come.
How long I've been alive.
How distant now seems Clyde Street, Island Bay.

Grandad smoked De Reszke cigarettes;
I had my scooter and my box of paints.
But I seem to be reluctant to write more,
as if allergic to my own capital.

*Is this where reticence begins?*
*Are continence and silence on the cards?*

## BITS BOX #1

Paris. London. Maximal New York.

But I stay here. I
do. Never quite achieving
escape velocity.

*

Mammoths in blue meadows

Pearls and coffee grits and bloodied gauze

*Don't say a word*
*while we dance with the Devil*

# YOUNG ELLIOT

I don't know it yet, but I'm in for a treat this morning: the charming flash of verbal delinquency.

Elliot hails from Liverpool, and I like Liverpudlians; he has an interest in film and is keen to make his first short movie right here in Wellington. Meanwhile, he's working as a barista at a place I frequent.

Taking a scheduled break from his duties within, he joins me at my table outside the café. And Elliot brings to the party a banana and a bottle – a bottle of bottled water.

"Hi," he says.

"Hello."

"You"ve been to the library?"

"I have."

"It's a good library."

"It is indeed. In many key respects."

Young Elliot eats his banana thoughtfully; I smoke the perfect rollie I've just rolled. "There's absolutely no need," I say.

"No need for what?"

"No need for you to be buying bottled water. Not in New Zealand, like."

"I know. It's just . . ."

"Just what?"

"It's just that I need the bottle itself, fuck it. I mean, I can't drink out of my hands like a cat."

# THE BLACK AND THE WHITE

1

Dice and chalices.
Harry Styles' outrageously good new song.

2

The famous neurosurgeon's never had
his own brain scanned. "I don't want to see
the shrinkage and atrophy that come with age."

3

I seem to have run out of luck
(my writing life has slowed to a nervous crawl),
but I pay for my latte
with an optimistic smile
and an action-packed assortment of shrapnel.

4

Shrinkage. Atrophy.

The neurosurgeon doesn't want to see
the green and the blue,
the yellow and the red,
the black and the white
of his own ancient brain.

5

*Curious pedantries*
move the whisky priest.

In a letter to Stephen Murphy, I write this:
"Do you ever make the sign of the cross?
I sometimes cross myself in a semi-prayerful way,
like a Spanish shepherd
watching a spaceship land."

6

One's duty, in the end?

One's duty in the end
is to get oneself dead somehow.

## BAD FOOT

My neighbour's tree has grown,
become more dense; no longer can I see
the red light on the hill.

*

I'm delaying, really.
Delaying's what I'm doing.
Delaying finding out
whether or not I've got
a broken bone in my foot.
(I rather think I have,
and I'd rather not know about it.)

*

I've been alive for aeons.
I've been alive for a very long time.

Trams of red and cream
ran through my childhood.
Island Bay was perfumed by burning leaves
(incinerators smoked in slow backyards),
and the city reeked of the sea
(Wellington was still a truly *maritime* concern).

## CHOSEN

I'm sitting outside the Victoria St Café (coffee, cigarette, my usual table) when a passing dog stops at my feet and gazes up at me with bright black eyes.

"He wants to say hello," his mistress tells me. "Would you mind terribly?"

"Not at all," I say, and give the soulful pooch a gentle roughing-up.

"He does this," says the woman.

"?"

"Each and every day, at some point on our walk, he stops and lets me know that this is today's person, the party he wants to be introduced to."

Only in the quietest moments
does it make itself heard,
atomically sublime and self-sustaining:

the ping of my own existence,
ping of my own existence,
ping of my own continuing existence.

# Index of titles

# Index of first lines

236

237

# Index of books